Coaching and Mentoring

2nd edition

Practical conversations to improve learning

Eric Parsloe and Melville Leedham

KOGAN PAGE

London and Philadelphia

Scottish readers should be aware that, in order to simplify the text, the author has referred only to NVQs. In nearly every respect, these are the same as their Scottish equivalent, SVQs.

Publisher's note

First edition 2000
Second edition 2009
Reprinted 2009

120 Pentonville Road
London N1 9JN
United Kingdom
www.koganpage.com

525 South 4th Street, #241
Philadelphia PA 19147
USA

© Eric Parsloe and Monika Wray, 2000
© Eric Parsloe and Melville Leedham, 2009

ISBN 978 0 7494 4365 8

British Library Cataloguing-in-Publication Data

A CIP record for this book is available from the British Library.

Library of Congress Cataloging-in-Publication Data

Parsloe, Eric.
    Coaching and mentoring : practical conversations to improve learning
/ Eric Parsloe and Melville Leedham. -- 2nd ed.
       p. cm.
    Includes bibliographical references and index.
    ISBN 978-0-7494-4365-8
    1. Mentoring in business. 2. Employees--Coaching of. 3.
Organizational learning. I. Leedham, Melville. II. Title.
    HF5385.P27 2009
    658.3'124--dc22
                                                              2008042680

Typeset by JS Typesetting Ltd, Porthcawl, Mid Glamorgan
Printed and bound in Great Britain by MPG Books Ltd, Bodmin, Cornwall

Contents

Introduction and acknowledgements

The first edition of this book was sent to the publishers on New Year's Eve 1999: the cusp of the new millennium. This edition was completed only some eight and half years into that millennium, but in a very different world of coaching and mentoring. Indeed, the pace of change has been so rapid and our own learning has been so hectic and continuous that we had difficulty in deciding when the manuscript was ready to be sent.

So we're conscious that, in a sense, we are only really stopping to draw breath and share our experiences with you before our learning journey continues once again. We recognize that we're still in the early stages of the revolution in thinking and understanding of how people can be helped to adjust and adapt to the increasing pace of our changing world and the increasing relevance of coaching and mentoring to that process.

Change and difference are a constant theme of this book and this second edition has a different writing team too. My co-author Melville Leedham and I have been both coaches and mentors to each other and I freely acknowledge that without Mel's constant commitment, and at times forcible encouragement, this manuscript would probably not have been completed for another eight and a half years! More important, Mel's research abilities and wide practical experience have meant that we've been able to explore and share developments in coaching and mentoring in greater scope and depth than a single writer could ever have managed.

Equally important has been the contribution of other team members. Elaine Patterson has significantly expanded the chapter on 'Helping people to learn how to learn' with the case study of her own journey, as well as contributing to the other chapters. Morgan Chambers has made a specialist contribution to understanding the ontological approach and Laura Parsloe, now a highly qualified psychologist herself, has persuaded a somewhat reluctant father to recognize the immense contribution that the fields of psychology, psychotherapy and counselling make to the understanding of our subject.

Thanks are also due to our grammar and style editor Xanthe Wells, our graphic consultant Linda Jane James, our colleagues and candidates from The Oxford School and, of course, to our personal and ever patient coaches and mentors Kate Parsloe and Patricia Leedham.

The main message of this book is that while coaching and mentoring can make substantial impacts on many aspects of people's lives and therefore require a deep understanding of people's behaviour and learning habits, they are in essence simple and practical activities. They are both very similar, or indeed almost identical, conversational processes that aim to help and support individuals to take control and responsibility for managing their own learning and development. In that sense they are age-old concepts with a new meaning, application and relevance in the modern world.

We all engage in conversations on most days of our lives, so our aim has been to keep to a simple and practical conversational style and we invite any of our readers who wish to continue the dialogue to contact us.

Eric Parsloe
eric@theocm.co.uk

1

From marginal to mainstream

At the start of the 1990s, you could hardly find a single book on either coaching or mentoring in the library of Templeton College, Oxford University's only management college at that time. Eight years into the new millennium, Templeton's librarians would now need a very large removal van to carry all the books, journal articles, news stories and internet references to our subject.

In the world of work and the broader social community, a rich variety of examples of successful applications of coaching and mentoring abound. It has truly been a transition from highly marginal activities to a mainstream focus of interest for professional institutes, management schools, corporate and community policy makers and anyone interested in people development. We are clearly in the middle of an 'intellectual revolution' with these activities and it is not surprising that there is still confusion over definitions and language. In the next few years, coaching and mentoring will, we predict, have become so clearly defined as a recognized profession and integrated into work and community life that they will be described routinely as simply 'the way we do things round here'.

Before we look at coaching and mentoring in more detail, we will first sketch a 'big picture' review of the trends, developments and influences of this explosion in activity.

THE MANAGEMENT AND ACADEMIC 'INFLUENCERS'

Our interest in the potential for both coaching and mentoring came from our own experiences of corporate life and the management writers (who were largely from the United States) of the 1980s. It was impossible to read the new thinking on issues like 'process re-engineering', 'total quality management', 'customer service excellence', 'employee empowerment' and 'the learning organization' without recognizing that the days of the traditional management science of command and control were numbered. The notion of coaching began to enter the language of people management and development literature, either implicitly or sometimes explicitly, in accordance with one of Blanchard's situational management styles.

The 'Situational leadership model' was developed by Paul Hersey and Ken Blanchard in the 1960s. The model comprises four quadrants, depicting the simple concept of the four different styles of leadership that a manager may need to adopt in any given situation; see Figure 1.1. One of those quadrants is called 'coaching'.

Figure 1.1 Blanchard and Hersey's 'Situational leadership model'

Hersey and Blanchard's use of the term 'coaching' did not have its current meaning, however: by coaching they meant a way of leading and persuading staff to adopt a manager's solution to the situation.

The US writer with the greatest early impact on the emerging profession of management coaching in Britain was most likely Tim Gallwey in his *The Inner Game of Tennis* (1974). His simple proposition that all great tennis players needed a coach to maintain their high levels of performance was a metaphor and message that was easy to relate to the management of people's performance at work. Gallwey made this message even clearer in *The Inner Game of Work* (2000).

Gallwey's philosophy that 'Performance = Potential minus Interference' was accompanied by the message that a coach's job was primarily to release the self-knowledge and potential that everyone possesses. The key to this was to develop greater self-awareness and a sense of self-responsibility in the performer. Again, these are messages that were in tune with the emerging new thinking about management and organizational performance.

Since 2000, a number of UK universities and some in Australia have pioneered programmes leading to formal academic qualifications. Oxford Brookes University was the first to offer a Master's Degree in Coaching and Mentoring Practice; Middlesex University offered a Master's Degree with a strong psychological emphasis and Sheffield Hallam University also built on its long involvement with mentoring research. Anthony Grant in Australia has been widely published, advocating the need for an evidence-based approach to academic research. One positive aspect of this increasing academic involvement has been a rapid advance in respectable research-based evidence and a recognized body of literature that many consider an essential requirement for the establishment of a genuine coaching and mentoring profession.

THE SPORT COACH 'INFLUENCERS'

Not surprisingly perhaps, it has been the famous 'sports-coaches-turned-management-coaching-gurus' who were the most visible group in shaping the early thinking and approaches to applying coaching to the workplace. Among the leading exponents were John Whitmore, former champion racing driver; David Hemery, former Olympic medallist; and David Whitaker, former Olympic hockey coach. Towards the end of the 1990s, the former tennis player Myles Downey teamed up with The Industrial Society (later renamed the Work Foundation) to form a 'School of Coaching' for high-flying managers. More recently, the former Olympic swimming gold medallist, Duncan Goodhew, joined up with the leading sports psychologist, Professor Graham Jones, and created a successful coaching company. Appropriately named Lane 4, this has helped to further consolidate the connection between sports coaching and a notion of 'best practice management'.

The medium most commonly used by this group to convey their messages is highly stimulating and memorable training courses. Here practical examples of sports coaching are used to relate to the world of work. The analogy between high achievers in sport and work has fostered the belief that it is possible to develop 'great coaches' who can help produce 'extraordinary results'. However, John Whitmore's book *Coaching for Performance* (1997, updated 2002) remains an inspiring call for a change of management philosophy. Like many pioneers before him, he has faced a growing number of other 'influencers' who challenge the sports coach approach.

The basis for some of the challenges is that the skills required to be a successful sports person are far narrower than those required to manage, for instance, a busy call centre, the intensive care ward of a large hospital or a pharmaceutical processing plant. Thus it has been claimed that the approaches and techniques are not easily transferred from one environment to the other. Indeed, to suggest that they can be easily transferred simply results in raising false hopes and expectations.

Another challenge to this school of 'influencers' relates to the difference in motivation between sport, which has a combination of personal competitiveness and pleasure, and the world of work where many, if not most, people's motivation is a mixture of reluctance, fear and resistance to change. Apart from the natural high achievers, it is claimed that the sports coaching approach often produces little real change in behaviour and performance. While we can all develop our self-awareness, most people don't aspire to be Olympic champions at work.

Despite the challenges, it remains true that this rather narrow and simplistic approach to work-based coaching continues to be a widespread basis for many training programmes, producing results that satisfy a particular segment of the market. However, John Whitmore has more recently continued his intellectual journey into the realms of the psychological and spiritual areas of transpersonal coaching, which he views as a natural evolution from his initial ideas.

THE HUMAN RESOURCES PROFESSIONAL 'INFLUENCERS'

The Chartered Institute of Personnel and Development (CIPD) has more than 130,000 members in the UK and is the main professional body for those involved in the corporate world of human resources and development. In that role it has taken a leading position in influencing the development of coaching and mentoring in the UK, conducting regular surveys of activity that are accepted as authoritative indicators of activity. In 2004 the CIPD reported that 78 per cent of the survey's respondents now state that they use coaching as part of their learning and development activities, and 57 per cent acknowledged an increase in using it over the past few years (with a further 20 per cent reporting a large increase). In addition:

- 99 per cent agreed that 'coaching can deliver tangible benefits both to individuals and organizations';

- 93 per cent agreed that 'coaching and mentoring are key mechanisms for transferring learning from training courses back to the workplace';

- 92 per cent agreed that 'when coaching is managed effectively it can have a positive impact on an organization's bottom line';

- 96 per cent agreed that 'coaching is an effective way to promote learning in organizations'.

In the 2006 survey, 72 per cent claimed that coaching was the prime driver used to increase productivity. Subsequent surveys continue to show strong evidence that coaching is not being seen as a panacea, but rather as an essential and valuable feature of a modern organization's learning and development strategy. This is indeed strong evidence that coaching and mentoring are now mainstream and no longer marginal activities.

THE COUNSELLING, PSYCHOTHERAPY, PSYCHOLOGY AND PHILOSOPHY 'INFLUENCERS'

As coaching and mentoring has become more widespread, it has inevitably brought practitioners from other 'helping' disciplines into the arena, who believe that their traditional methods and approaches are highly relevant. This has certainly increased and enriched the debates and involvement of many more people in the formation of the emerging profession. We recognize the importance of this contribution and, in Chapter 5 'Awareness of individual differences', we explore this contribution in more detail.

However, the widening of the debate has also had a somewhat negative and confusing impact. It is our opinion that too many people from the different disciplines are now trying to over-complicate the world of coaching and mentoring. The current market place is swamped with a multiplicity of apparently conflicting brands and terminology: NLP, co-active, ontological, buddy, transpersonal, solutions-focused – the list goes on. Differences between the brands sometimes relate to a specific context but more often to some theoretical or academic influence that is of little relevance to the process.

THE PROFESSIONAL BODY 'INFLUENCERS'

Inevitably, as coaching and mentoring have become so widespread, there has been pressure to form networks and associations that can lead to representative bodies bringing some coherence into an emerging profession in the UK. At the same time existing professional bodies have recognized this need and a possible opportunity for them to extend their membership and influence.

The CIPD, representing the human resources professional, has played a leading role but it has increasingly recognized that it needs to collaborate with others rather than try to dominate the debates. The British Psychology Society (BPS), which has several different groups within its membership, has taken a more defensive attitude and has emphasized the case for psychologists leading the debate. The British Association of Counsellors and Psychotherapists (BACP) has adopted a position somewhere in between the other two bodies.

Far more influential in framing the debates have been the new representative bodies that we discuss in more detail in Chapter 9. The International Coach Federation (ICF), initially largely North American, now has more than 12,000 members in a range of countries around the world. They are complemented in North America by coaches mainly from the corporate sector who have formed the World Association of Business Coaches (WABC). In Europe the European Mentoring and Coaching Council (EMCC) has taken a lead in developing standards and qualifications for both coaching and mentoring in the corporate world and the community. In the UK and many other European countries, national associations for coaching have been formed and energetically promote the benefits of coaching to help their largely individual membership. In the UK a group of psychotherapist coaches formed their own association, the Association of Professional Executive Coaching and Supervision (APECS).

The existence of these various bodies with their own agendas initially added considerably to the confusion in the market. Fortunately common sense and recognition of mutual interests have led to an increasing level of cooperation, which hopefully will lead to the creation of a single unifying organization.

SO WHERE DOES THAT LEAVE US?

For buyers of coaching services, it can be tempting to give up trying to navigate this swamp of theoretical models and obtuse jargon, but if one is patient, steps back and asks what all these people are doing and why, it is really pretty straightforward. If you watch coaching or mentoring in action, in most cases what you would see is simply two people having a conversation, and we all have conversations every day.

A closer analysis of these conversations would establish that they are often very focused, confidential and ideally voluntary conversations that are quite structured and follow a process that helps learning to occur, allowing performance to improve and potential to be realized. In truth, they are a very specific type of conversation and not everyone, in management for instance, is used to having the patience and skills to help people learn in this way.

It is now generally accepted that people learn in different ways and therefore it is also common sense to accept that there is no single correct theoretical approach that should be followed. Clearly, the motivation behind coaching and mentoring in education or, say, for drug users, is quite different to that of high potential young managers in large businesses. We explore 'Helping people to learn how to learn' in Chapter 4.

The words 'coaching' and 'mentoring' have a long traditional usage and interpretation but, in the late 20th century, the activities they describe have taken on new dimensions in corporate, community and social life across the world. This has led to considerable confusion over the appropriate modern definitions. In our opinion this is mainly because of the confusion between:

▌ *what* it is and does;

▌ *why* it is used;

▌ *where* it has come from;

▌ *how* it is done.

What *it is and does*

Both coaching and mentoring are conversations that generically follow a simple, although slightly different, four-stage process to help and support people to take responsibility for managing their own learning and change.

Why *it is used*

The main purpose of both these conversations is either to improve skills or performance, or to realize individual potential and personal ambitions for the future – or any combination of these.

Where *it has come from*

Modern coaching and mentoring have been shaped by a range of influences and schools of thought as well as Western and Eastern cultures. As such, these conversations take from this rich tradition ideas of what it is to be human and how to help people realize their innate potential.

How *it is done*

These conversations take place in so many varied contexts and for so many purposes that there is no one correct way of 'how to do it'. However, successful conversations imply the building of a relationship that includes a degree of mutual trust and commitment.

There is a considerable overlap in the knowledge, competences, skills and techniques that can be used by the individual coach-mentor. However, there is also considerable flexibility to choose an appropriate style of intervention to suit the context in which the conversations take place, varying from a highly non-directive style to a highly directive style, and from theoretical or philosophic standpoints to pragmatism and common sense. Opinions vary strongly on these issues between the purists and the pragmatists who believe interventions can often be a combination of styles, even during a single conversation.

As pragmatists ourselves, we have chosen the term 'coach-mentoring' for the modern definition of these conversations. Similarly, we believe that the range of coaching and mentoring styles that can be chosen are most simply understood as related to a continuum of situations, as shown in Figure 1.2. This illustrates the typical objectives and duration of the relationship for each broad purpose and the most appropriate intervention style for each situation. Professional and effective coach-mentors need the knowledge, competences, skills and techniques to be able to adjust their style seamlessly as the situation in which they are working changes, even during the same conversation.

Throughout the rest of this book we will use the term 'coach-mentor', as well as the term 'learner' (rather than coachee, mentee or client) since we believe we are all involved in the learning experience. We will also continue to keep our ideas and suggestions as simple and practical as possible, believing with Leonardo Da Vinci that: 'Simplicity is the ultimate sophistication.'

In that spirit we will advocate a number of 'practical tips of simplicity' derived largely from our years of experience in the world of work and the community.

Figure 1.2 Situational coach-mentoring continuum

Simplicity Tip 1

Success comes most surely from doing simple things consistently

We have met very few people who could not become good, competent and useful coaches and mentors. The key to success is not to over-complicate the roles or to erect unrealistic and unnecessary barriers and expectations. Our 'Tips of simplicity' reflect an approach that provides the basis for successful coaching and mentoring relationships. To achieve real sophistication, however, we must also recognize that 'simple' does not mean 'easy': in fact the opposite is probably true.

Simplicity Tip 2

First agree what you are going to talk about

Many effective coaching and mentoring conversations can happen spontaneously and informally but, if the purpose is to effect serious learning and lasting change, a series of conversations over a longer timeframe are more likely to produce results. In this case, it is important to be very clear at the start of the relationship exactly what the ground rules are going to be so that you can both stay focused and disciplined. This phase of the relationship has become known as the 'contracting' phase: not in the sense of a written document but in the sense that all those likely to be affected by the conversations understand what is being aimed for. This can lead to a three- or four-way contract if managers or representatives of a sponsoring organization are involved, as they often are the paymasters.

Simplicity Tip 3

Make sure you meet

By far the most common reason for coaching and mentoring schemes to fail is that the busy coach-mentor, volunteer or manager, doesn't find the time to meet with his or her learners. Of course, time pressures are intense on everyone and have arguably grown significantly in recent years. Yet we all have the same amount of time available to us. So the real issue is what we choose to do with our time and what tools we can use to help us find the necessary 'extra' time. Here technology, such as the telephone, or more recently computer-based communication techniques, have a real role to play.

The tool most commonly used to help manage our time is, of course, the diary. We strongly advocate the use of some form of learning and/ or planning diary in which both the coach-mentor and learner commit to each other to make contact at a specific time and on a particular day each month. The simple act of writing the commitment down increases the likelihood of it happening.

But be honest: if you don't intend to keep the commitment, don't write it down. No manager, in particular, can advocate the need for others to take personal responsibility for improving performance if he or she is not prepared to take personal responsibility for finding the time to meet. It is as simple as that.

Simplicity Tip 4

Keep it brief

Time is precious so there is no point in wasting it. Formal coaching and mentoring sessions in the workplace can be productive if they take between 30 and 75 minutes. If they are shorter you don't really have time to become focused, but if sessions take longer they run the real danger of straying into the realms of counselling or therapy sessions.

We acknowledge the need to be flexible in applying this rule. Sometimes situations are too stressful to be rushed. Sometimes learners need time to unburden themselves. Certain types of people simply don't respond easily to time-pressured situations. So the coach-mentor has to be willing to be both flexible and patient.

This is where the 'make sure you meet' tip applies. Regular meetings allow the coach-mentor to vary the length of the meetings to take account of the occasional stressful or difficult session. But after, say, three of these necessarily lengthy sessions, we would advise turning to another specialist for help. Coach-mentors cannot be expected to be able to handle every situation and they become potentially dangerous if they think they should.

Simplicity Tip 5

Stick to the basic process

At the most basic level, coaching and mentoring sessions are one-to-one meetings where the learner talks about issues he or she chooses and the coach-mentor listens and asks questions. However, the conversations need focus, structure and, especially, good time-management. Sticking to a simple process that ensures this happens is therefore crucial:

▊ Ask the learner either to come prepared with his or her agenda or spend the first few minutes agreeing it.

▊ Ideally you should both write it down and then manage the time spent on each item.

▊ Agree that taking notes is purely optional.

▌ Try to make certain you both write down any action points that the learner decides he or she genuinely wants to commit to (and make sure it is the first item on the agenda for the next meeting).

▌ Agree the date and time for the next meeting.

The process really is as simple as that. If you adhere to it you are signifying to the learner that:

▌ These are *not* management, operational or performance review meetings.

▌ These are *not* appraisal meetings that require documentation for the Personnel Department.

▌ These are *not* disciplinary meetings.

▌ These *are* meetings that are controlled by the learner and focused on him or her and his or her needs and ambitions.

▌ In most situations the contracting phase should have ensured that they are also meetings that are completely confidential.

Simplicity Tip 6

Develop the 'ask, not tell' habit

Most managers quickly develop the habit of 'acting as managers are expected to act'. This will vary from organization to organization depending on the prevailing culture (and probably on how many different training courses managers have attended!). It will also depend on age, sex and personality type; but you can be pretty sure that there will be 'management-style' habits.

You can also be reasonably sure that many managers will be unfamiliar with acting as coaches and mentors, and not likely to fully accept the underlying philosophy that letting go of control opens the potential for higher performance. The idea that good coaching and mentoring means moving quickly away from a 'directive' to 'non-directive' style is one of the most difficult barriers for managers to overcome.

Developing the 'ask, not tell' habit is a vital new habit for managers and the community volunteer mentor to learn. Spelling it out as a formula of '75 per cent asking questions, 20 per cent giving answers and only 5 per cent sharing suggestions', is another way we have found to help some people adapt their style. However, it is probably the constant repetition and reminder of this tip that is the most certain way to get it established.

Even managers who can accept this philosophy intellectually have real problems with applying it. Faced with the pressures of accountability for both positive financial and customer satisfaction short-term results, many managers tend to revert to more traditional command and control styles and techniques. We appreciate that to expect otherwise is unrealistic and unsympathetic.

Simplicity Tip 7

Remember it's all about learning

Another attitude barrier that busy people have to surmount is the concept of 'self-responsibility for learning'. A deeply ingrained habit, indeed preference for some people, is to associate 'learning' with classroom or training course activities. Traditionally, organizations have taken primary responsibility for developing the skills and knowledge of their employees. They have also taken responsibility, in many cases, for planning whole careers. The role of the line manager has all too often been largely confined to conducting the annual appraisal and agreeing a 'wish list' of training courses.

Coaching and mentoring sessions on a monthly basis, discussing a personal development agenda determined by the learner, will represent a major change of behaviour for a large number of managers. In our experience only about 30 per cent of any management population will, in the short term, be open to being persuaded to try to implement this kind of change in their routines. Even then it will take three to four months before the benefits become apparent; but benefits there certainly will be and patient, persistent trust in the process will be rewarded.

One of the benefits most likely to be noticed first is the real cost-effectiveness of coaching and mentoring compared to the results of sending people on courses away from the workplace. An hour of on-the-job learning and development conversation that can be immediately related to current applications saves a great deal of time and money. Persistently reminding people that 'it's all about learning' and simply pointing out the real-life benefits, helps to make coaching and mentoring become the habitual 'way we do things around here'.

Simplicity Tip 8

Expect to gain yourself

Benefits from coaching and mentoring are not a one-way flow in the direction of the learner, the employing organization or the wider community. Coach-mentors almost always benefit too by learning new techniques for getting results from the people they work with. There are also the less tangible benefits of the feedback from more highly motivated and appreciative colleagues or from those who have made real breakthroughs in managing their previously difficult life situations.

Coach-mentors should not be embarrassed to acknowledge the 'self-interest' expectation. Indeed we would positively encourage them to adopt this win–win attitude. Equally, it is worth emphasizing that our definition of the overall purpose of coaching and mentoring includes 'helping people to become the person they want to be'. This opens the possibilities of rewards from outside the immediate environment of the organizational setting.

Simplicity Tip 9

Be aware of the boundaries

Even in the community context where extreme patience is required, it is still important to keep a sense of proportion about the time spent in a programme of coaching and mentoring dealing with stressful and difficult issues. These sessions may be therapeutic but they should not become therapy.

The workplace is a robust environment and is possibly becoming even more demanding and unforgiving. We accept that counselling and therapy have an important role to play here but we believe that it is a job for specialists. Recognizing the boundaries of 'normal' stress and anxiety from those behaviours that border on clinical dysfunction is an important skill for the non-professional to develop. Making people aware of these boundaries should be an essential element in any coach-mentor development programme. While always being prepared to listen, attempting to help beyond the boundaries of your competence can be really dangerous.

Simplicity Tip 10

Don't try too hard

Inexperienced coach-mentors who have an idealistic and enthusiastic desire to help people learn and change often make the mistake of expecting immediate results and become disappointed and disheartened with their own lack of competence or insufficient tools and techniques.

It is important to recognize that the coach-mentor is joining the learner on a journey that has often been in progress for many years already. While most people have the potential to change attitudes or behaviours, it usually takes time to achieve. Coach-mentors are basically providing the time and space for that to happen. They need to trust in the process and be content to simply be there for their learners, bringing their own personality, values and confidence in themselves to the situation. It is not necessary to try too hard because it really is as simple as that.

Simplicity tips – summary

1. Success comes most surely from doing simple things consistently.
2. First agree what you are going to talk about.
3. Make sure you meet.
4. Keep it brief.
5. Stick to the basic process.
6. Develop the 'ask, not tell' habit.
7. Remember it's all about learning.
8. Expect to gain yourself.
9. Be aware of the boundaries.
10. Don't try too hard.

But please remember that simple is not easy! To remind you of Da Vinci once again 'Simplicity is the ultimate sophistication.'

2

Models of coaching and mentoring

The purchasers of coaching and mentoring have become more discriminating since the first edition of this book in 2000. One of the questions they are now fond of asking potential suppliers is along the lines of: 'What is your own model of coaching?' The answers they tend to get often reflect the academic, psychological or philosophical training of the supplier. Alternatively, they may get the confident response, 'Well, mainly the GROW model.' GROW, of course, is not a model of coaching but instead a powerful mnemonic for sequencing questions in a range of situations.

Due to the potential confusion and variation of definitions and models, in this chapter we will explore a number of our preferred models of coaching and mentoring.

TOWARDS AN IDEAL MODEL

'Mentor' was the name of a character from Greek mythology who was a wise and trusted adviser or counsellor. Until recently, the word kept that meaning: it is a word that is regularly used by politicians, sports people, actors and other performers to describe the person whom they chose as a role model or someone who had a significant early influence on their professional careers.

'Coaching', on the other hand, only became widely used over the last two to three hundred years. It was initially used to describe the activity of helping transport a person's knowledge and skills towards a higher level, mainly by a form of teaching or tutoring. In the 20th century, however, it became most widely applied in the context of sport and performance.

We have already established that coaching and mentoring in the context of the 21st century is a dynamic and expanding workplace and community activity. It is most likely that the definitions proposed by any of the recent writers on coaching and mentoring are still reasonably accurate in describing what happens in practice in many day-to-day situations in 2008 (see the Appendix for a selection).

Organizations have been moving at different speeds towards more sophisticated and effective implementation of coaching and mentoring. The most important point, however, is not that everyone has to agree on a single definition, but that everyone in a specific organization should know the definition that applies to their particular situation. In many cases, organizations are using the words interchangeably. We believe that it is much more important that the purpose and the output of the relationship are clear and agreed, rather than focusing on an exact and academic definition of the terms.

To comprehend the modern definitions, we suggest it is helpful to discuss the idea of 'ideal models' of the activities for both individual professionals and managers acting as coach-mentors. However, we recognize that all coach-mentors are likely to behave in the way that seems appropriate to them in their particular situation. Describing an ideal model, therefore, is not to suggest that it is the only way to do it, but rather that it is a benchmark to compare to your real-life practice and from which you can create your own model. Our purpose is to find some sort of common language, but any model or framework that suggests a pattern of behaviours needs to be applied with pragmatism and common sense, being driven by the needs of the learner and by his or her unique context.

Finding a way out of the confusion

With so many definitions available, it is easy to understand why so much confusion exists, but we suggest that there is a generic four-stage model that can be applied to most coaching and mentoring relationships. Like all processes, it requires each stage to be properly completed if the whole process is to work most successfully. Missing out stages or concentrating on one at the expense of the others can lead to confusion and poor results.

We are aware that our own preference for focusing on four-stage process models is not shared by some theorists and academics, who prefer to emphasize the interpersonal skills, styles, philosophical and psychological aspects of the relationship. Nonetheless, our experience, as we outlined in the previous chapter, suggests that it is more helpful to accurately understand 'what' a coach-mentor is supposed to do, before moving on to understanding 'why' and 'where' it came from and 'how' it might be done.

This chapter focuses on a model or framework tailored for the world of corporate and professional life that applies equally to the internal coach and the external coach. The following chapter will focus on adapting this model to suit the rise of community mentoring and life-coaching. However, we are aware that there is also a lot of overlap and that such neat distinctions can easily become distorted. For example, many people coming for business-focused coaching may want and need to move into the more personal areas of what has traditionally been called life-coaching, and vice versa. One should therefore bear in mind that such frameworks and approaches need to be blended and applied with common sense to their individual situation.

THE GENERIC COACH-MENTORING PROCESS

The four stages of the generic coach-mentoring process are:

1. Analysing for awareness of need, desire and self.

2. Planning for self-responsibility.

3. Implementing using styles, techniques and skills.

4. Evaluating for success and learning.

The model can be illustrated using the diagram in Figure 2.1, which helps to emphasize that this is not simply a linear process but one that is in constant motion within the whole and with considerable overlaps between the stages.

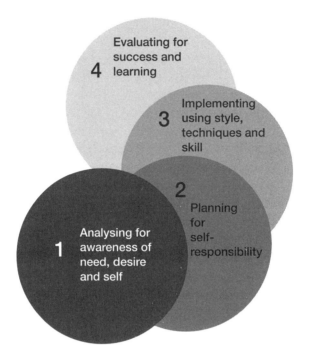

Figure 2.1 The four stages of the generic coach-mentoring process

Stage 1. Analysing for awareness of need, desire and self

Coach-mentoring can only start when learners develop an awareness of the need and desire to improve their performance or change the way they have been doing things at work, as well as in life generally. Without a genuine recognition of need and desire, it is almost impossible to change behaviour. Like the old saying that you can take a horse to water but you can't make it drink, the coach-mentor needs to help the learner develop this awareness because you cannot coach-mentor someone unless he or she actually wants to be helped to change.

Learners develop awareness in a number of ways. One way is to use psychometrics or personality profiling, but it is often easier and more practical to ask questions that analyse their current performance and compare it to the level that they would like to move towards. Having clear standards or personal competences to aim for is very helpful, particularly when developing a specific skill. Using self-assessment exercises as the basis for subsequent conversations is a powerful technique for developing awareness.

At this stage it is also important to check the learning style preferences of both the learner and the coach-mentor. For the learner, this will provide insights into ways of learning about themself that he or she will naturally prefer and therefore probably find easier and more enjoyable. For the coach-mentor, it is important to recognize any differences in preferences between themself and the learner. This will help to guard against the natural tendency to suggest learning opportunities that may work well for him or her but which may be inappropriate for the learner. It will also help to spot situations where any obstacles to learning may be caused by the learner's choice of methods rather than an inherent difficulty with the content of the learning. This stage is sometimes described as the 'contracting stage' because it should ideally involve all stakeholders in the relationship to be completely aware of the mechanics and desired outcomes.

Stage 2. Planning for self-responsibility

It has long been argued that effective learning and development only really occur when the individual takes personal responsibility for the outcome. The planning stage of the coach-mentoring process is the opportunity for the learner to begin to exercise responsibility. There is a temptation to ignore this stage, particularly if the coach-mentor or learner has an activist learning style preference and is impatient to 'get on with it'. Busy managers are also inclined to ignore this stage and often prefer the informal 'Let's do it on the run' approach.

The danger of missing out on this stage is that the coach-mentoring can become ad hoc, ie unstructured and failing to focus on the real issues. If self-managed learning is the preferred approach, then planning is absolutely vital.

Coach-mentors cannot, and should not, attempt to impose learning programmes. Learners must be actively involved in the decision making, although some compromises between an ideal programme of learning and what can realistically be afforded will often be necessary. However, experience suggests that, in the work context, agreeing a Personal Learning Plan (PLP) of some kind with the learner's manager ensures that the necessary time and space in the working day will be made more readily available.

A successful PLP for any context needs to answer these key questions:

∎ What is to be achieved?

∎ How will it be done?

∎ Where will it be done?

∎ When will it start and end?

∎ How will it be measured?

∎ Who will be involved?

∎ Who needs to agree the plan?

In many organizations, individuals are already encouraged to have PLPs. In a minority of instances, the PLPs cover any topic that interests the learners, like a foreign language or horticulture for instance, because the organization believes that encouraging the development of the learning habit is more important than precisely what is learnt. Few organizations are likely to follow this enlightened approach, however, and most will probably insist that a PLP is clearly linked to business objectives as well as to individual aspirations.

Unlike the traditional annual appraisal Personal Development Plan (PDP) that is often, in practice, only a long wish-list, to be most effective a coach-mentoring PLP should focus on only one or two specific development goals over relatively short timeframes, such as the next three months. It is important too, that any development goal in the PLP should be SMART (Specific, Measurable, Achievable, Relevant and Timeframed). This simple mnemonic is often only paid lip-service in practice, but it can be a very powerful technique for ensuring real focus. The PLP should be reviewed at least on a monthly basis and thus could become an integral part of the performance management process.

Stage 3. Implementing using styles, techniques and skills

Coach-mentors need to use implementation styles and techniques that are appropriate to the situation in which the learner is operating. The appropriate style and technique also need to be employed with the right balance of personal coaching skills appropriate for the particular stage of the process. Coach-mentors need to be comfortable and competent to move up and down the support challenge spectrum between directive and non-directive. They also need to provide a safe space for exploration, discovery and true learning to take place as the learners face their professional and personal challenges. The most important of these skills are generally: observant listening, effective questioning and giving feedback. We will look at several coaching techniques, as well as these skills in more detail later (see Chapters 7, 8 and 9).

Opportunities for coaching arise on many different occasions during the working day and it is important to seize them when they occur. This leads some people to argue that there is little need for formal planning and that the best coaching is informal, relying almost entirely on questioning and immediate feedback. Our experience suggests, however, that creating awareness and a sense of personal responsibility requires time for proper planning, if serious change and development are to be achieved. In truth, the two approaches are in fact complementary: while formal awareness and planning are important, informal coaching can take place whenever the opportunity arises.

Our main concern about the informal approach is that once the initial enthusiasm wears off, it very often leads to no coach-mentoring at all. The most common reason for this is that people fail to find the time to do it. A more formal approach that sets aside an hour a week or month in both party's diaries is much more likely to ensure it happens. Formalized timetabling may sound boring, but in a hectic working environment it often produces results, especially when the manager has already signed off the PLP. Formality also often ensures regular opportunities to monitor and review progress on the PLP and to reinforce new learning.

Stage 4. Evaluating for success and learning

Many people confuse monitoring with evaluating. Monitoring is the essential activity of regularly checking that progress is being made in implementing the PLP. Evaluating is the activity of reviewing the PLP once it has been completed. It is a one-off activity involving the coach-mentor, the learner and any other interested stakeholder. The key questions are:

▌ Were the measurable development goals achieved?

▌ Did the different components of the PLP work in the sequences they were designed to?

▌ What changes, if any, were made to the PLP and why?

▌ Was the PLP cost-effective and did it justify the investment?

▌ Were there any unexpected benefits?

▌ What did we learn that would lead us to do things differently next time?

▌ Is there a need for a new PLP to improve performance still further?

Clearly, if the answer to the final question is 'Yes', then the whole process needs to start again. This is a likely outcome since performance needs to improve continuously.

MENTORING

To understand more fully the developments in the 'models debate', let us focus for a while on mentoring. Mentoring, like coaching, can happen in many different contexts or environments:

▌ Business-to-business, where the main thrust is on economic regeneration and where a mentor from a large organization works with one from a small or medium-sized enterprise.

▌ Business-to-enterprise, where, for example, organizations like the Prince's Youth Business Trust has mentors to guide young 'starters' in business who have received grants from them.

▌ The UK government regularly announces programmes similar to business-to-enterprise, but where the learner may have special needs in gaining access to employment.

▌ Special needs and community projects, where the mentoring is more personal and designed for individual needs and where matching the mentor and learner may be critical.

▌ Business-to-education, where business people volunteer to work with headteachers, teachers and students.

▌ Graduate or undergraduate mentoring, where more experienced graduates help to guide or counsel students through different stages of their studies.

Corporate mentoring roles are often designed to support specific groups:

▌ new recruits;

▌ graduate trainees;

▌ women;

▌ ethnic minorities;

▌ disabled or disadvantaged individuals;

▌ individuals facing a career change, redundancy or pre-retirement;

▌ people with a specific desire and motivation to manage their own learning and development.

It is hardly surprising that no single definition or model uniformly fits all these different contexts. We need to try to understand both the differences and the similarities, but we suggest that there are three broad primary types of mentor:

1. *The corporate mentor* who acts as a guide, adviser and counsellor at various stages in someone's career, from induction through formal development to a senior management position and possibly into retirement.

2. *The qualification mentor* who is required by a professional association or government-sponsored agency to be appointed to guide candidates through their programme of study, leading to a professional qualification or a National Vocational Qualification (NVQ).

3. *The community mentor* who acts as a friend, expert adviser or counsellor to individuals in a wide range of situations where the individual may be disadvantaged or in an actual or potentially distressing position.

Examples of these three types of mentor can, of course, be found in many organizations. Sometimes all three may be found simultaneously in a single large organization. In this section, we will discuss both the 'corporate' and 'qualification' mentor. The 'community' mentor is a significant development that we deal with separately in Chapter 3.

The words used to describe each stage of the corporate and qualification mentoring process are different from the generic coach-mentoring model. Here the key stages are:

1. Confirming the personal learning plan (PLP).

2. Encouraging the self-management of learning.

3. Providing support during the PLP process.

4. Assisting in the evaluation of success and learning.

The wording of the stages also reflects the different roles, responsibilities and accountabilities of a mentor from that of a coach or coach-mentor. Mentors in the workplace are rarely a learner's direct line manager whereas a coach very often is. The corporate and qualification mentoring process can be illustrated graphically, as in Figure 2.2.

Stage 1. Confirming the personal learning plan

Final responsibility for the personal learning plan lies with the learner and his or her manager. A mentor may be involved at any stage during the preparation of the PLP, but his or her role is simply to help to confirm by providing guidance, access to information and acting as a 'sounding-board'. The mentor has no direct responsibility or accountability for the learner's performance although, in the qualification context, he or she is often required to follow set guidelines.

The mentor has to prepare for the role by analysing, identifying and anticipating the likely needs that the learner will have in achieving his or her learning and development goals. The mentor will need to be sensitive to all the circumstances within which the learner is operating, including his or her personal beliefs, capabilities, aspirations and learning style preferences.

The mentor needs to encourage the development of self-awareness in the learner by showing how self-assessment and honest open questioning can help to achieve this. One of the key areas where a mentor may help is by checking that all the learning and development

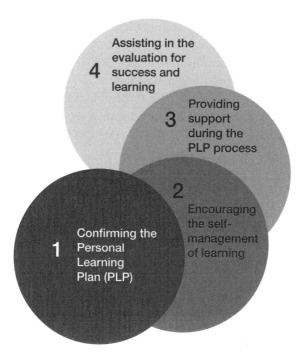

Figure 2.2 The four stages of the corporate and qualification mentoring process

goals meet the SMART criteria. The mentor can also usefully draw attention to the need to set goals with short and realistic timescales. Even a long qualification programme is more successfully tackled in short manageable stages.

As with the coach-mentoring process, this stage is sometimes described as the 'contracting stage' because it should involve all stakeholders in the relationship to be completely aware of the mechanics and desired outcomes.

Stage 2. Encouraging the self-management of learning

One of the characteristics of a good PLP is the extent to which it allows for self-management of the process. However, not all learners will have sufficient experience to manage the implementation of the PLP. By asking probing questions, the mentor's greater experience should allow him or her to encourage learners to think ahead and anticipate some of the administrative aspects of implementing the PLP. The mentor can also provide a useful service by giving clear explanations and reminders at the appropriate moment of the range of support options that may be available.

One of the most critical aspects of the mentoring role is to ensure that the day-to-day working relationship between the learner and the line manager is not compromised by the mentor's activities. Learners should be encouraged on all occasions to work out their own solutions to any problem they have with their line manager or other colleagues. A mentor is a 'sounding-board', not a trouble-shooter and any suggestions or advice should be given as options to consider rather than instructions to act upon. Conversations need to be in confidence so that a genuine level of trust can exist. Only in the most extreme situations should a mentor intervene directly. Adopting a genuinely objective, confidential and impartial role may not always be easy in practice, but it is essential.

Stage 3. Providing support during the PLP process

As soon as the PLP starts to be implemented, the mentor needs to be available to provide support. In minimal practical terms, this means agreeing a schedule of meetings as frequently as seems necessary. It is also useful to agree methods for arranging impromptu meetings or contact to deal with any urgent and/or unforeseen difficulties.

The way in which the mentor provides guidance and information is critical. Timing, pace and level are obviously important, but the danger of imposing the mentor's natural preferences must be guarded against. Avoiding bias of all kinds and remaining objective, while at the same time fully involved, is not always an easy balance to strike.

Mentors will sometimes be asked to provide advice and make suggestions. The key here is to ensure that advice and suggestions are given only when requested and not imposed on the learner in an attempt to appear helpful. The mentor is definitely not expected to be the source of all knowledge and information, and he or she should be quite willing to direct learners to alternative and perhaps more appropriate sources.

A key role for the mentor is to help learners to deal with mistakes and setbacks which, in some line management relationships, may result in blame, guilt and feelings of inadequacy. The mentoring relationship should be non-judgemental and 'risk-free'. This allows the mentor to help the learner to treat mistakes and setbacks as real learning opportunities. Properly handled, these situations are often rich learning experiences.

At all times, the mentor should try to build self-confidence and motivation in the learner in order to develop a positive attitude and a will to complete the PLP.

Stage 4. Assisting in the evaluation of success and learning

There is a distinction between regular monitoring of progress and final evaluation at the end of the PLP. A mentor's role is to encourage the learners to arrange formal evaluations with their line managers or qualification supervisors.

Helping the learners to prepare for a formal evaluation is a useful mentoring function. Reminding them of the value of self-assessment and peer-assessment of performance standards is particularly helpful. Mentors can use reflective questions to help learners to analyse the causes of any barriers to learning that occur, as well as quantifying the benefits that were gained by themselves and the organization during the PLP process.

Formal mentoring relationships usually come to an end. Most often this occurs when a learner changes job or with the achievement of a professional or vocational qualification. Ending a relationship is often not easy. Celebrating success and recognizing the mutual benefits gained are important. The mentor should make a special effort to encourage the learner to continue to set new development and career goals. Agreeing to maintain interest and contact in the future is a positive note to end on.

To summarize the similarities and perhaps subtle differences between coaching and mentoring process models, Table 2.1 might prove helpful. It would seem that this corporate mentoring process is very close to the process that many external professional executive coaches would use to describe the services that they provide. This merely serves to underline the pragmatic use of the term 'coach-mentor'.

A 'CONTRACTING' PROCESS MODEL

A quite different process model that can be applied to all situations is the 'contracting' model or competence framework. The National Occupational Standards issued by the UK Qualification and

Table 2.1 Generic models of coaching and mentoring

	Professional and Business Coaching	**Corporate and Qualification Mentoring**
Stage 1	Analysing for awareness of need, desire and self	Confirming the Personal Learning Plan (PLP)
Stage 2	Planning for self-responsibility	Encouraging the self-management of learning
Stage 3	Implementing using style, techniques and skills	Providing support during the PLP process
Stage 4	Evaluating for success and learning	Assisting in the evaluation of success

Curriculum Authority (QCA) and the Professional Standards issued by the European Mentoring and Coaching Council (EMCC) have helped us to define a process for agreeing a 'contract' with stakeholders in the relationship. This can apply as part of a wider framework of competences for both coaches and mentors. To help understand this important process you might like to assess yourself against our model, shown in Figure 2.3.

THE MANAGER OR LEADER AS A COACH-MENTOR

Another quite different model that can prove valuable is that of the manager or leader as coach-mentor, which some people advocate should be based on a model derived from sport. For instance, coaching Olympic performers to reach even higher standards is a very sophisticated activity. The coach, who is often not at the same performance level as the performer, has to recognize that the performer has total control over performance. The Olympic coach can operate in a non-directive style and focus largely on the mental attitude of the performer rather than his or her basic skills and techniques. Coaches of top performing teams and of stars in the performing arts also are encouraged to follow this pattern.

On the other hand, it is argued that most coaching in corporate life is undertaken by line managers rather than external professional coach-mentors. Some believe that the same non-directive approach to

SELF-ASSESSMENT

CONTRACTING

Score yourself

1 to 10 scale, where 10 = excellent and 1 = very poor

How well do I prepare the contract with stakeholders?

- ■ I ensure that all stakeholders understand and agree the expectations of the process before starting

- ■ I work with, and agree with all stakeholders, the objectives and outcomes of the work

- ■ I agree the framework for completion to include end date, number of sessions, review dates, location, pricing and terms and conditions

- ■ I clarify the role and responsibilities of the stakeholders in the process

- ■ I establish with the learner and stakeholders the implications of the process on their time, workload and potential changes in behaviour and attitude

- ■ I agree the boundaries, especially of confidentiality between the learner, the stakeholders and myself

How well do I create the coaching contract with my learners?

- ■ I determine that there is an appropriate match between my style and the needs of the learner before proceeding

- ■ I ensure the contracts are made with full consultation with and agreement from all relevant parties including who, specifically, will be involved in the review process

- ■ I agree with the learner a code of practice that defines the boundaries or our working relationship, including confidentiality and expectations of each other in terms of honesty and commitment to act on agreed outcomes

- ■ I help the learner to identify and deal with the time pressures and any other potential issues that may affect the process

- ■ We agree a schedule of sessions, where they will take place, how long they will last and the method of communication (face-to-face, telephone, e-mail, etc)

Figure 2.3 Contracting self-assessment model

transferring control as in sport should always apply in the workplace too. The reality of applying that approach is illustrated in Figure 2.4. Many managers find it difficult to move quickly along the management control styles axis towards a non-directive position. Partly this is because some managers are locked into a traditional hierarchical command and control management style and are ill-suited and personally uncomfortable with changing style.

Sometimes too, the culture of their organization and the structure of the jobs that have to be done force them towards a directive style. For instance, in the situation of a simple, repetitive, task-oriented department with a high turnover of staff or a heavy reliance on temporary or short-contract employees, a manager-coach may be constantly forced into situations where a directive style is the only appropriate one to adopt. Similarly, in situations of great urgency, a fire alarm for instance, there is no time for a period of reflective questioning!

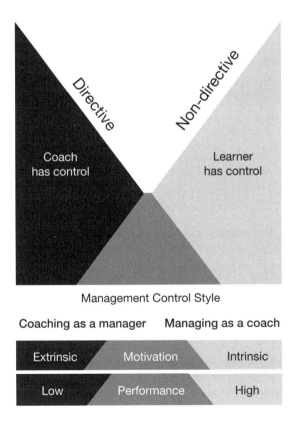

Figure 2.4   Manager or leader as a coach-mentor model

It is also true that where managers are held closely accountable for immediate results with severe penalties for failure, it is difficult for them to take the risk involved in letting go of control and trusting the performer to take responsibility for improving performance. This is a very real problem for many managers, and has been made worse with the increases in workload and stress that have resulted from many experiments with re-engineering, the impact of new technology and organizational restructuring or mergers. These pressures help to explain why many coaches and learners are probably operating at around 25–30 per cent along the axis towards a non-directive style. There has been a lot of talk about sharing control and empowerment, but often there is a real and understandable reluctance to put it into practice.

Of course, there is a fundamental contradiction in this reluctance to change style. Experience shows that higher levels of performance from individuals and teams are more often achieved when people are given greater control and responsibility. So the desire and pressure for ever higher performance standards are often, in practice, frustrated by a reluctance to risk releasing control. This frustration is likely to contribute to increased stress levels for managers.

For organizations wishing to develop the necessary 'positive coaching culture', there is no alternative but for managers to move rapidly down the coaching style axis toward the non-directive position. This implies a change in management style away from 'coaching as a manager' towards 'managing as a coach'. In persuading managers to try to adopt a new style it will be equally important to acknowledge the practical difficulties that many of them might face.

A management coaching style

'Style' is used here to describe 'the manner in which the coach-mentoring is delivered', although some writers use the term 'style' to describe different roles or types of coaching. However, these are not based solely on a psychological analysis of those involved. Coach-mentoring styles can more usefully be based on a continuum that ranges from situations where the learner is completely inexperienced to situations where the learner is highly experienced and capable, or in situations requiring very different outcomes.

When working with someone who is completely new to a situation or needs to develop a specific new skill, it may be appropriate to adopt a directive, almost instructor-like, style. When dealing with an experienced high performer, like an Olympic athlete or Chief Executive, it is more appropriate to adopt a non-directive style and rely mainly on questioning and feedback skills. Experience shows that the more rapidly a coach-mentor can move from a directive to a non-directive style, the faster an improvement in performance or behaviour change will be achieved. The simple explanation for this is that as you move along the axis towards a non-directive style the more control and responsibility is transferred from the coach-mentor to the learner.

A COACH-MENTORING COMPETENCE MODEL

To assist you further, you may care to complete the self-assessment exercise in Figure 2.5, which is based on yet another model to help you to establish your current levels of competence as a coach-mentor. Often our own perceptions are more critical than others, but we may also be unaware of some aspects of our behaviour. Self-assessment is a powerful technique for raising awareness and providing an agenda for open dialogue with your colleagues and your coach.

Summary

In this chapter, we have asserted that there is currently no consensus on terminology in the field of coaching and mentoring and that the current terms and definitions may continue to change as the 'revolution in thinking' continues. We have also noted that theoretical models are useful only if they are used to help us to understand new ideas or concepts; hence the benefit of designing models for ourselves that suit our own specific situations.

Although we have advocated generic four-stage models for coaching and mentoring, applications and experiences of coaching and mentoring are likely to differ in different international and cultural contexts. And, of course, we are all still learning!

SELF-ASSESSMENT

COACH-MENTORING COMPETENCE

Score yourself

1 to 10 scale, where 10 = excellent and 1 = very poor

- How well do I prepare the contract with stakeholders?
- How well do I create the coaching contract with my learners?
- How effective am I at establishing rapport?
- How effective am I at building and maintaining the relationship?
- How effectively do I manage sessions?
- How good am I at helping to clarify goals?
- How well do I help to explore options to achieve these goals?
- How good am I at ensuring the goals align with the organizational needs?
- How well do I support the development of an action plan?
- How well do I support implementation of the action plan?
- How well do I facilitate the review process and measurement of progress?
- How well do I monitor the overall coaching process?
- How well do I manage the conclusion of the relationship?
- How well do I conclude the contract with stakeholders?
- How appropriate is my approach to the learner?
- How good am I at listening?
- How good are my questioning skills?
- How well do I give and receive feedback?
- How flexible am I?
- How well do I maintain 'business focus'?

Figure 2.5 Coach-mentoring competence self-assessment model

3

Community mentors and life-coaching

In this chapter we will explore in more depth two of the perspectives mentioned in Chapter 2: 'community mentoring' and 'life-coaching'. There is a significant and growing sector of coaches and mentors whose prime focus is not on improving the business performance of their learners; instead, the focus seems to be helping people to learn how to cope with life's challenges, to be better able to change what can be changed and to accept positively what cannot be changed.

The purpose of many community mentoring programmes is to help those who, for whatever reasons, are currently excluded from or have never been in the world of work. This includes those in schools or in prisons, those with physical or mental disabilities and many other forms of social exclusion. In the health care sector, there are examples of using mentoring not only in the traditional field of developing staff but also in helping patients to cope with chronic illness. For the purposes of clarity, we have split this chapter into two perspectives: 'community mentors' and 'life-coaches'.

WHAT IS LIFE-COACHING?

'Life' is probably one of the most familiar prefixes to 'coaching', thanks to the media and popular coaching celebrities. A recent web search found 27 million references to life-coaching. UK television programmes such as *What Not to Wear*, *How to Look Good Naked* and even *Supernanny* all have one thing in common: trying to improve a person's self-image or self-esteem. In 2005, a glossy magazine was launched in the UK called *Psychologies* with each issue containing articles and features on life-coaching. There are also regular features on therapy, mental health and lifestyle. These examples suggest that self-improvement and some aspects of mental wellbeing are now acceptable topics of conversation.

Exactly when the term 'life-coaching' began to be used is not clear. It first became popular in the 1950s alongside the emergence of humanistic psychology, the focus on human potential and self-help. In those early days, life-coaching tended to be associated with non-conformity, a challenge to conventional values, dropping out, unworldliness, etc. In some circles this is still the image conjured up when life-coaching is mentioned in contrast to business coaching.

However, in recent years there appears to have been a great deal of overlap with business coaching. In both the approaches used and coaching issues addressed, both might borrow from 'inner game' principles and NLP (neuro-linguistic programming), and cover areas such as career coaching, work–life balance and confidence building. This section seeks to explore this growing area of the profession by looking at the context of life-coaching and some tools and approaches.

Context

The term 'life-coaching' is, for some, synonymous with 'coaching' and often used interchangeably with 'business coaching'. When searching for a definition of life-coaching the ones usually quoted cover coaching in a generic sense; if the word 'life' were removed it would be difficult to identify the unique aspects of 'life-coaching' from any other form of coaching.

Grant (2001) attempted to make a distinction between what he called personal or life-coaching and coaching in the workplace:

> Personal or life-coaching is a solution-focused, results-orientated systematic process in which the coach facilitates the enhancement of the coachee's life experience and performance in various domains (as determined by the coachee), and fosters the self-directed learning and personal growth of the coachee.
>
> Workplace coaching is a solution-focused, result-orientated systematic process in which the coach facilitates the enhancement of work performance and the self-directed learning and personal growth of the coachee.

We discussed business coaching in Chapter 2 where the focus is on addressing the development needs of the client required to achieve business outcomes rather than a focus on the personal or career goals of the person being coached. Life-coaching clients tend to be individuals who are self-funding (ie not receiving external coaching via their organizational sponsor, or via an internal coach) and therefore many of the potential conflicts of interest that can exist within business coaching are removed.

For the purposes of this chapter, life-coaching is taken to mean coaching that is geared totally towards achieving personal success and self-fulfilment, which goes beyond serving an organization's agenda. This allows far more scope for focusing on achieving the clients 'ideal life' that would not often come under the remit of business or workplace coaching. However, whatever description is used, the general consensus seems to suggest that life-coaching is personal coaching that is defined by the context in which it takes place rather than the skills, tools or techniques that are employed by the coach.

The common contexts in which life-coaches operate typically include:

▌ confidence and self-esteem;

▌ career transitions;

▌ relationships;

▌ dreams and aspirations;

▌ getting your life in order;

▌ health and physical wellbeing.

Confidence and self-esteem

Often people who present themselves for life-coaching want to feel good about themselves: they want to be more confident in social groups and be confident to go out, meet new people and build acquaintances into friends. Generally this will be because they have low self-esteem, high self-doubt and consequently lack confidence. Life-coaching can be effective for tackling negative thoughts and lack of self-belief. Sessions might include such practical activities as making small talk and/or giving speeches and presentations.

Career transitions

Within an organization it is often difficult to discuss wanting to change careers or even saying you are dissatisfied with your current job. Someone considering a major career change or starting his or her own business might consult a life-coach. Redefining or exploring core values might be part of this process. Here people will feel freer to openly discuss issues about their job or working for the organization that they could not discuss with anyone at the same employer.

Relationships

This may focus on problems or dilemmas with their life partner or other members of their family. Business coaching can only legitimately enter these personal areas when they have a direct impact on the work performance of the individual. Life-coaching can help people work through family and partner difficulties or simply help them cope with life's challenges.

Dreams and aspirations

Sometimes people who have worked hard for many years, striving for material success, try to take stock of their lives. They find themselves saying things like: 'There must be more to life than this.' They may look around at their lives and find that work no longer satisfies them or they want to 'do more with their lives'. Life-coaching can be helpful for finding new direction and purpose and helping people work out the important things in their life. Looking to have more fun, enjoyment or adventure are all topics that might be difficult to discuss with a line manager or business coach.

Getting your life in order

Another aspect of people's lives where life-coaching can be helpful is in creating some order and discipline. Many of us would benefit from 'de-cluttering' our homes or even our minds, using our time more effectively and generally becoming better organized. Managing our finances can also be included in this context, such as living within our budget, increasing our savings, reducing our outgoings, etc. Life-coaching can be useful for those suffering from procrastination or lack of focus.

Health and physical wellbeing

Many people seem to be obsessed about their weight and/or their body shape. Recently the trend for healthier eating has become more common, with more people striving to live a generally healthier life-style, including giving up smoking. Life-coaching can be helpful in providing the motivation to begin and encouragement to stick to a specific exercise regime, diet or quitting smoking.

An increasingly hectic and stressful life can be another reason why someone would seek a life-coach. Stress can have an adverse effect on a person's health and lead to many illnesses. A report released in May 2006 by the UK Health and Safety Executive shows that just over a fifth of UK workers are concerned about work-related stress. Half a million people a year report that stress levels are making them ill. Life-coaching can be effective in helping to establish a better work–life balance. The case study below shows how the UK National Health Service is recognizing the potential benefits of coaching for some groups of patients.

NHS 'health coaches'

One example of what could be classed as a form of life-coaching is that of 'health coach' within the UK National Health Service.

In 2005, there were 17.5 million people in the UK suffering with long-term conditions with the expectation that by 2030 this will more than double. In particular, Type 2 diabetes related to obesity is expected to grow by 54 per cent and hypertension by 28 per cent.

In February 2004, Pfizer Ltd and Haringey Primary Care Trust launched an innovative programme designed to provide individualized support and coach-mentoring for 600 patients within the London Borough of Haringey suffering from diabetes, heart failure and coronary heart disease.

The aim of this project was to investigate the benefits to patients of a telephone-based and technology-supported coach-mentoring and self-care programme using a patient-centred disease management model in England adapted from a successful disease management approach from the United States.

The programme was born out of growing recognition of the potential benefits for patients and the NHS of improving chronic disease management. As Jill Lewis (Care Manager, Development Lead, UK Pfizer Health Solutions) comments: 'Self-care is about empowering individuals to take actions to maintain their health. Support for self-care involves increasing the capacity, confidence and efficacy of the individual for self-care by providing a range of options.'

A team of dedicated care managers or 'health coaches' provide regular coaching interventions for patients based on their individual needs. The care managers, all qualified nurses, use decision support software in a systematic telephone-based coaching and coordinated care service. Each health coach is a qualified nurse, with a dedicated case load of 150–200 patients, who has been trained to provide coach-mentoring and support.

Through this regular communication and support, patients have become more successful in managing their condition and have improved their clinical outcomes and quality of life, while reducing the demands on local health services. The results of the evaluation of the programme were released in the spring of 2006.

Patient satisfaction levels included:

- 90 per cent patient satisfaction with the health coach;
- 70 per cent improved their confidence regarding health decisions;
- 61 per cent thought it enabled more useful discussion with doctor.

The impacts on the individual patient included:

- improved health outcomes;
- people felt more confident to manage their condition;
- improved quality of life with greater independence;
- improved life expectancy.

Potential benefits to the NHS included:

- 40 per cent decrease in the number of primary care consultations;
- 17 per cent decrease in outpatient visits;
- 50 per cent reduction in Accident & Emergency Department visits;
- hospital admissions and length of hospital stays halved.

Perhaps this comment from a patient on the health coach programme sums up what life-coaching and community mentoring is all about: 'The programme has helped me, I am a different person since being on the programme, especially my diet and food intake. The care manager is very good and helps me to be healthy and happy.'

As you can see from the above examples, life-coaching can cover any or all aspects of a person's life. Sometimes clients seek life-coaching for a specific issue, such as health, relationships, finances, or career transition. On the other hand, it may be something more ambitious like creating a new life for themselves, while sometimes it's to hold on to and appreciate more what they've already got, or to regain something that seems lost. Others are drawn to coaching by a general dissatisfaction with their life or a sense that something could be better. Perhaps a more appropriate title in some of these contexts would be to call it 'lifestyle' coaching.

Approaches

Some key tools and approaches used in life-coaching are familiar in other areas of coaching, such as the 'Wheel of life' and variants of GROW, described in Chapters 6, 7 and 8. However, while the business coach borrows freely from the plethora of tools, models and psychometrics arising from the world of business, life-coaches tend to fill their toolkit from much wider areas such as pop-psychology, astrology, self-help and even hypnotherapy. It is worth noting that some of the approaches used can reflect quite specific and unconventional worldviews or approaches, such as the combination of martial arts with hypnosis, or crystal healing, and would be more likely to hold appeal for like-minded clients.

Life-coaching sessions tend to be shorter than business coaching: typically half an hour to an hour rather than one to two hours. Also, the frequency of sessions is often shorter: weekly for life-coaching as opposed to monthly for business coaching. There appears to be a very high proportion of life-coaching done over the phone and often the participants never meet the coach.

There also appears to be an emphasis on prescriptive structure and process and the benefit of programmes with a set number of steps or stages, such as:

▍ five top tips to make it real;

▍ five steps to conquer your fear;

▍ five ways to put the passion back;

▍ seven rules of success;

▍ change your life in seven days.

Life-coaching tends to be based on the following principles:

▍ Define your life purpose. If your family wrote an epitaph about you today, what would they write? What would you like them to write?

▍ Be positive. Make sure the goals are described in positive terms and about things you want to achieve, not about things you want to stop or eliminate.

▍ Look to build on your personal strengths, not weaknesses. Don't allow any strength to be discounted or negated.

▍ Take personal responsibility for immediate challenges and problems. Don't focus on other people's problems or blame them for your situation.

▍ Failing to plan means you are planning to fail. Decide on a series of relevant and achievable developmental actions that will contribute towards your goals.

▍ Celebrate success and be proud of your achievements. List your achievements in positive terms, not as partial failures.

COMMUNITY MENTORING

Now let us examine community mentoring in some detail: it will soon become clear how different the context is from the world of work and qualifications as illustrated by the models in the previous chapter. The process may have many similarities, but the values and the behaviours required are quite different.

There appear to be at least four distinct forms of community mentoring emerging within the UK; they are discussed below. The distinctions are based on the nature of the objectives for the supportive relationship and the importance given to achieving those objectives, in addition to the importance attached to the social aspect of the relationship.

1. Befriending

Befriending is the term used to describe the role of volunteers who provide informal social support. The primary objective of these relationships is to form a trusting relationship with the individual over time, usually to reduce isolation and to provide a relationship where none currently exists. In some cases, there may be additional stated objectives at the start of the relationship such as a growth in confidence or his or her increasing involvement in community activities. The success of the relationship is not dependent on these objectives being achieved, but they are seen as a potential benefit of befriending over time. The Mentoring and Befriending Foundation (MBF) provides guidance and support to organizations and practitioners involved in mentoring and befriending. As the UK national strategic body, MBF also works to influence policy and practice in the sector and across government.

2. Employment mentoring

Mentoring in preparing for employment is used where a school believes pupils are not achieving their potential and are capable of higher examination grades. Typically the borderline is between grades D and C since achieving the maximum number of grades A–C is a key measure for published school league tables in the UK. This form of mentoring is usually done by volunteers from local businesses who visit schools to increase the self-confidence of these 'borderline' pupils.

The purpose is to increase the pupils' appreciation of what companies expect of future employees and to give them the confidence and knowledge to access employment opportunities.

3. Positive action

Positive action mentoring targets people in what are considered to be oppressed or minority groups. This includes young people from a predominantly black or Asian ethnic community. This form of mentoring also includes encouraging young women to enter traditionally male-dominated industries such as engineering. A key tactic here is to offer positive role models from within the targeted community where the mentor is expected to make influential introductions, open doors and remove organizational barriers.

'100 Black Men' as an example of positive action mentoring

100 Black Men is a voluntary self-funded mentoring organization working in the UK through chapters in Birmingham and London. Its prime focus is African-Caribbean boys aged from 10 to 16 and young adults, but it also works with young African-Caribbean girls in the same age range.

The overall concept of 100 Black Men began in New York in 1963 when a group of concerned African-American men started meeting to explore ways of improving conditions in their community. These men envisaged an organization that would implement programmes designed to improve the quality of life of African-Americans and other minorities. They also wished to ensure the future of their communities by aiming an intense number of resources at youth development. These members were successful black men from all walks of life. Today the organization has grown to over 10,000 members in 103 chapters, which continue to strive to improve the quality of life in their communities and enhance the educational and economic opportunities for young people.

100 Black Men of Birmingham (UK) was the first international chapter of the organization, formed in 1997 by a group of professional black men who were concerned about what was happening in their city. The 100 Black Men of London was formed four year later in April 2001 by a small group of concerned and committed men who were also aware

that if change were to come about in their community they would have to be proactively involved in that process.

The 100 Black Men of Birmingham (UK) are men who have achieved some business or personal success, or are striving to achieve that success. They have been working in various schools in the city for several years and in December 2005, members developed a mentoring programme for the African-Caribbean prisoners at HM Prison Stafford. The President, Nigel Gardner, said:

> All members give their time and efforts voluntarily and currently are experiencing great personal satisfaction in seeing how these efforts are positively impacting on the young men and women on our programmes. 100 Black Men of Birmingham believe in the promise of our youth and we exist to mentor our youth where we can. We will encourage and guide our youth to realize their potential in positive ways. What they see is what they can be. The African-Caribbean community in Birmingham faces many challenges; by mentoring we hope we are playing a part in moving the community forward, and developing our future leaders. We strongly believe that through our collective efforts and experiences, we can make a difference. At 100 we encourage our youth to realize their own potential and to think of ways in which they in turn can help the community. All of us can and should give something back.

4. Social inclusion

Engagement mentoring targets those people considered to be dis-affected with society or who are socially excluded. These are generally young people who have become disconnected or disengaged from the core institutions of school and work and sometimes have already been involved in the criminal justice system. The key purpose of this form of mentoring is to help these people re-enter the education system and/or the employment market.

The 'Fifteen Foundation' as an example of engagement mentoring

'Fifteen' was created in London by Jamie Oliver in 2002. Millions watched the UK Channel 4 programme that followed Jamie's ups and downs as he got to grips with the challenges of handling 15 tough young people who thought they might want to be chefs. 'Fifteen' London continues to be a very successful restaurant and recruits 20 youngsters each year. There are now 'Fifteen' establishments in Cornwall, Amsterdam and Melbourne and the Fifteen Foundation has a goal to grow 'Fifteen' into a global brand.

The Director of the Fifteen Foundation, Liam Black said in 2007:

'Fifteen' exists to reach out to young people who are often disregarded in society – the focus all too often is on what's wrong with them. 'Fifteen' focuses on what's right with them, providing opportunities and support through which they can find and develop the best in themselves. This involves a unique encounter with food and Jamie Oliver's inspiring approach to cooking and service. But 'Fifteen' is so much more than a chef training project. Food and cooking are the means to the end. The purpose is personal transformation for each young person. After graduation, our young move on a lot more confident, having made some lifelong friends and with a great chance of making a career at the top of the restaurant business.

We work with young people who often come from troubled families, who have 'failed' at school and who have experienced homelessness, drug and drink problems, have been ensnared in the criminal justice system, and consequently have low self-esteem, self-defeating patterns of behaviour, and social networks that serve to keep them locked in to poverty and underachievement. We are under no illusions that we can 'fix' them. We cannot sort out family problems, undo a criminal record or compel them to give up smoking weed. What we can do is provide them with more choices, open doors to new networks and opportunities and invite them to step through, helping them develop new skills to deal with their old problems.

The chefs and senior managers have clearly been carrying out an informal but very effective mentoring role with these young people. In 2006, they decided that they needed to build an even stronger culture of mentoring and coaching throughout the business. They took six members of staff through a six-month course to become qualified mentors and others to become qualified to teach mentoring to the franchise partners around the world. The programme has had a positive impact among the staff, increasing active listening and other supportive behaviours.

'I am really enjoying it and actually get as much out of the sessions with my three mentees as I hope they do,' said Liam.

There is an additional form of community mentoring we need to include in this chapter: 'learning mentors'. These differ from the previous examples as they are in paid employment specifically as mentors rather than a voluntary role alongside their proper jobs.

THE LEARNING MENTOR

We have already mentioned the voluntary role of 'preparation for employment mentor', which first started in the UK with the Business-Education Partnerships in 1993. Although this voluntary scheme still continues, in 1999 the UK government announced the creation of a new full-time post in the state education system – the learning mentor as one of the three main strands of its 'Excellence in cities' policy. This was a package of measures designed to improve inner-city education in the UK. Over the years, this initiative was widened to cover what became known as 'Excellence clusters'. This development was possibly the most significant endorsement of the power of mentoring as a new approach to learning and as such, the creation of these full-time professionals justifies the exploration of this role in more detail.

The original target was 1,000 learning mentors in place. Since then, the learning mentors concept has spread rapidly and by 2005 there were estimated to be around 12,000 working across the primary and secondary education sectors. However, the total number is believed to be significantly higher since there are many directly funded posts not included in this estimate.

Learning mentors are also established as part of the new Children's Workforce, supported through the new Children's Workforce Development Council (CWDC). The CWDC was set up as part of the UK government's commitment to workforce reform in the Green Paper, 'Every Child Matters', and is responsible for the implementation and support of the current government's 'Children's workforce strategy'. The establishment of this important new occupational group has been formally recognized in the UK through the National Occupational Standards for Learning, Development and Support Services (NOS LDSS) issued by the Qualification and Curriculum Authority (QCA).

These learning mentors are generally salaried staff who work with school and college students to help them address barriers to learning. With the objective of providing a bridge across academic and pastoral support roles, these mentors aim to ensure that individual students engage more effectively in learning and so achieve appropriately. They are now seen as a key ingredient in many schools and colleges to improve the achievement levels of students.

The official description of the work is to provide 'support and guidance to children, young people and those engaged with them, by removing barriers to learning in order to promote effective participation, enhance individual learning, raise aspirations and achieve full potential'. The work of the learning mentors falls into these broad areas:

- Providing a complementary service to existing teachers and pastoral staff in school and to others providing services to children and their families outside school (such as Social and Youth Services, the Education Welfare Service, the Probation and Careers Service and business, community and voluntary workers) so enhancing existing provision in order to support learning, participation and the encouragement of social inclusion.

- Developing and maintaining effective and supportive mentoring relationships with children, young people and those engaged with them, targeting help on those who need it most in deprived areas, especially those experiencing multiple disadvantages.

- To raise standards and reduce truancy and exclusion in the target areas, and to help local education authorities and schools to make accelerated progress in their achievement of truancy, exclusion and other relevant targets.

- Working within an extended range of networks and partnerships to broker support and learning opportunities, and improve the quality of services to children and young people.

There is clear evidence that such schemes are proving effective, as the following three quotes confirm:

> Learning mentors are making a significant effect on the attendance, behaviour, self-esteem and progress of the pupils they support... the most successful and highly valued strand of the EiC programme... In 95 per cent of the survey schools, inspectors judged that the mentoring programme made a positive contribution to the mainstream provision of the school as a whole, and had a beneficial effect on the behaviour of individual pupils and on their ability to learn and make progress. (OFSTED, 2003: 46)

> Pupils receiving support from learning mentors were one and a half times more likely to achieve five or more examination results at grade A* to C than young people with similar prior attainment who had not been mentored. (Morris et al, 2004)

> Learning mentors are very skilled at helping students work through and overcome problems often from outside school, which are preventing them from learning. Through a combination of individual counselling and support sessions, group work, residential trips and after-school activities, they are help-ing students to achieve significantly higher grades than originally predicted. They are providing support for those students considered the most vulnerable. (Hanson School, Bradford, September 2005)

The 'person specification' used in recruiting the learning mentors highlights the differences in the way this type of mentoring is ex-pected to be delivered. The specification states that the key skills and competences for learning mentors would include:

▌ The ability to engage constructively with, and relate to, a wide range of young people and families/carers with different ethnic and social backgrounds.

▌ The ability to work effectively with, and command the confidence of, teaching staff and senior management within the school.

▌ Working with others, the ability to assess and review young people and family circumstances and plan appropriate responses, drawing on in-school and external advice and expertise where necessary.

▌ A proven track record of working with young people, and an ability to see a child's needs in the round.

▌ A desire to do something worthwhile for young people, to understand their needs and to gain insights into how they think.

▌ Knowledge of, and ability to work effectively and network with, a wide range of supporting services in both the public and private sectors; and ability to draw on a wider range of support, information, opportunities and guidance.

▌ Ability to identify potential barriers to learning and jointly engage in strategies to overcome these barriers.

▌ Ability to see the mentoring role as a long-term activity designed to achieve the goals in the learning action plan and not a quick fix/trouble-shooting role.

▌ Ability to engage in joint goal setting with the individual child as part of the learning action planning process.

▌ Have time and energy to put into the relationship.

▌ Be up-to-date with current 'know-how'.

▌ Possess competences in the skills of networking, counselling, facilitating and developing others.

▌ A willingness and ability to learn and see potential benefits.

This ambitious specification also required the creation of an infrastructure of contact and communication, not only among learning mentors, but with others working in the public and private sectors.

Unfortunately, there is a real debate about the domination by the so-called 'social worker/therapist lobby' of the discussions on the nature of the necessary skills development and professional standards required. But as Helen Fisher, Head of Staff Health Care at Birmingham City Council suggests:

> Personally, I agree wholeheartedly that in terms of community and learning mentors, there is no room for turf wars between the therapy/social work lobby. In fact the schemes have appeal by virtue of their distance from the professions, as for some individuals it must feel as if the authorities have dominated their lives.
>
> Community/learning mentors reinforce potential, not pathology or marginalization. Obviously the coach-mentor needs to be appropriately trained (in the broadest sense) in basic counselling/coaching skills and having a keen

awareness of ethics, standards and particularly boundaries are vital. In the context of the relationship, contingency plans need to be agreed in advance for providing support to mentors who have to deal with distressing life stories and events with ongoing support and development from supervision, which models the relationship they are themselves trying to create.

Mentoring forms compared

We believe there are many key elements to any successful community mentoring programme. But it is important to understand the challenges similarities and differences between 'corporate', 'qualification' and 'community' mentoring with greater clarity. Undoubtedly, the basic four-stage process model of analyse–plan–implement–evaluate applies here as in the corporate coach-mentor and the qualification mentor roles. For community mentoring, however, the differences in the language and behaviours required are perhaps best captured in a model on the following lines:

Stage 1. Gaining understanding and awareness.
Stage 2. Motivating for action.
Stage 3. Supporting the plan.
Stage 4. Reviewing and maintaining momentum.

The model is shown in Figure 3.1, opposite.

Stage 1. Gaining understanding and acceptance

Unlike the world of work where time needs to be tightly managed, the community mentor has to be prepared to spend as long as it takes to build a close rapport and gain a sense of trust and confidence in the learner, who is likely to be extremely uncertain. Projecting the right balance between empathy and firmness is not easy. The mentor also has to be able to provide access to a range of information and support agencies; establishing the boundaries between the mentor's role and that of other professionals is key. The issue of building trust needs to be handled in a way that demonstrates that the mentor is impartial: he or she has no hidden agenda and really believes that there is no right way of doing the things that the 'establishment' and those in authority are 'pushing'.

Helping the learners to develop a self-awareness and acceptance of their existing strengths and weaknesses is a similar requirement to

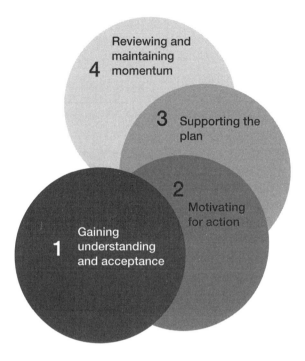

Figure 3.1 The four stages of the community coach-mentoring process

other types of mentoring. The style and tone of voice requires greater sensitivity than is perhaps acceptable in the more robust environment of the workplace. The credibility of the mentor 'having been there, done that and lived to tell the tale' can be very powerful in this instance. For example, a young teenage mother struggling to manage normal but unruly children may not respond well to someone who, although well-meaning, comes across as yet another 'expert' giving her instructions. However, someone who has been through a similar experience is more likely to encourage a positive response.

Stage 2. Motivating for action

Community learners often have a sense of personal inadequacy or feel they have already been labelled as 'failures'. Overcoming this negative self-perception and motivating them to construct an action plan to help to change their circumstances is no easy task, and the volunteer mentor can have a particularly valuable role here. Training for both mentors and their learners and other support is required. The most effective method is for the mentor to role-model the usefulness of keeping records, setting goals, reflecting on progress and making use of other support, supervision and training opportunities.

The key is a combination of firmness and encouragement with patience and empathy: undoubtedly, a difficult cocktail of skills to be mastered. Setting goals, for instance, often needs to be taken in very small steps and in a way that recognizes the huge difficulties some people have in mastering this discipline. Lack of patience and unrealistic expectations of the speed of progress are two of the main reasons for drop-out and failure. In this respect, the contrast with corporate mentoring is probably most vivid.

Stage 3. Supporting the plan

Having encouraged the learner to decide a plan of action that involves a gradual step-by-step route to a goal, the community mentor – unlike the other types of mentor – cannot simply sit back for a while and expect the learner to become a self-starter overnight.

A hand-holding role may sound patronizing, but being prepared to accompany learners on their first visit to an after-school activity, the library or government agency may be just what is required. Providing support during a plan often means just 'being there to talk' on a regular basis. The most common obstacles to achieving the goals arise from life circumstances outside a formal programme, and the personalized mentoring relationship can be used to work through personal and domestic issues. The danger for mentors who are too enthusiastic or too keen to be 'helpful' is that they may create a situation where the learner becomes too dependent on them. Striking the correct balance is not easy, and the availability of a mentor to the mentor (sometimes called a supervisor) can be invaluable in helping to manage this type of situation.

Stage 4. Reviewing and maintaining momentum

All programmes need to be monitored to review progress during the plan and to evaluate the outcomes at the end. Monitoring and reviewing is a constant process, but evaluation really takes place at the end of a programme or the completion of a plan.

In a corporate or qualification context, this may mean completing a skills development programme or being awarded a professional qualification. In a community context, the achievements may seem more modest, but are equally valuable. For instance, being able to open a bank account and to write your name on the cheques may be a huge success for someone who is severely dyslexic and who may feel he or she has been unfairly labelled as a failure by the education system. The need to celebrate these successes and at the same time to build motivation to set new goals is the same in all contexts.

A structure for a final evaluation session that has been found to work well is to ask the following sequence of questions:

- What did you actually do?

- What had you hoped to achieve?

- What did you actually achieve?

- Were there any unexpected learning points?

- How would you describe the personal benefits?

- What do you think you could do next to build on your achievements?

If the relationship has been successful, the chances of continuing progress, even without the formal involvement of the mentor, will usually be high.

THE EMERGENCE OF THE COACH-MENTOR

The challenge for both community mentoring and life-coaching is to create appropriate and relevant development programmes and take a broader approach to setting national standards and qualifications that effectively meet the variety of needs of the emerging profession. One aspect of these developments will be gaining agreement on the language and theoretical models on which the new standards are to be based. These need to be seen alongside other government initiatives: the aim of 3,000 business-to-headteacher mentors and the 1,000 volunteer business-to-business mentors, for instance. In our opinion these legitimize the role of 'community mentor'. The claim for the recognition of 'community mentors' alongside the 'corporate' and 'qualification mentors' as a profession is clearly strong.

Also, the enormous growth in life and lifestyle coaches seen in recent years and the blurring of the distinction between business coaching and life-coaching and indeed with the professional executive coach and executive mentor must be acknowledged. This blurring of distinctions strengthens our view that the new professionals can realistically call themselves professional 'coach-mentors' and acknowledge this spectrum of support roles and the overlap of skills, attributes and qualities needed by everyone involved.

In Chapter 2 we introduced a model to help us to understand the similarities and differences between 'professional and business coach-mentoring' and 'corporate and qualification mentoring'. In this chapter we add the extra context of 'community mentoring' to provide a full picture; see Table 3.1.

Table 3.1   Expanded summary model of coaching and mentoring

	Professional and Business Coaching	Corporate and Qualification Mentoring	Community Mentoring
Stage 1 (Awareness)	Analysing for awareness	Confirming the Personal Learning Plan (PLP)	Gaining understanding and acceptance
Stage 2 (Responsibility)	Planning for self-responsibility	Encouraging the self-management of learning	Motivating for action
Stage 3 (Action)	Implementing using style, techniques and skills	Providing support during the PLP process	Supporting the plan
Stage 4 (Reflection)	Evaluating for success and learning	Assisting in the evaluation of success	Reviewing and maintaining momentum

You will note that we have added another four labels to each stage of the summary process (see Figure 3.2), which gives an even simpler generic model that encapsulates our thinking.

Figure 3.2   The four stages of the coach-mentoring process

To help complete this chapter, you may care to do the 'Mentoring volunteers health check' in Figure 3.3. (Bear in mind that corporate and qualification mentors often volunteer for the role in addition to their existing jobs, while to a large extent community mentors usually volunteer for their role in their non-work time.)

SELF-ASSESSMENT

MENTORING VOLUNTEERS HEALTH CHECK

Tick the box as appropriate, where A=Definitely, B=Partially, C=Not at all

	A	B	C
■ Do you understand how mentoring differs from other roles you are asked to play in your organization?			
■ Do you really want to take on the role and are you willing to make the necessary time available?			
■ Are you comfortable in being asked to assess your own strengths and weaknesses and relate them to the learners' development needs so that you can guide them to other sources of help where it is appropriate?			
■ Are you sure that you can invest time early on in the relationship to establish rapport and a regular schedule for discussions?			
■ Do you know how to enable the learners to produce a realistic development plan, and ensure that it is 'signed off' by all the relevant people?			
■ Will you be able to keep the relationship on a professional level, particularly where there are differences in gender (sensitivity to potential misinterpretation in language and behaviour will be important in these situations)?			
■ Do you understand the distinction between counselling and advising, and whenever possible, will you encourage the learners to work out their own solutions with you acting only as a sounding board?			
■ Are you aware that you will be a role model, and that how you are seen to manage yourself in day-to-day situations will affect the relationship you have with the learners?			
■ Are you sure that the feedback you give will be clear, honest and constructive, and designed to build confidence and ongoing commitment in the learners?			
■ Will you be able to recognize when the time has come to end the relationship, and aim to end on a positive and supportive note by sharing the value you have both gained from the experience?			

Figure 3.3   Mentoring volunteers health check

4

Helping people to learn how to learn

We have asserted that the main purpose of coaching and mentoring is to help and support people to take control and responsibility for their own learning. It is important to explore this issue in some detail. It is a sobering thought to realize that up until the mid-1980s it was quite possible to be very successful in managing a business or community organization without even mentioning the word 'learning'. Certainly, that was our own experience.

For a growing number of people in the public, private and independent sectors, the concept of the 'learning organization' is now seen as an accurate blueprint of the way organizations will need to be structured and to behave in the 21st century. The blueprint may be visionary, but each organization – small, medium or large – will, it is argued, be required to build its own version if it is to be successful. Coaching and mentoring, we believe, will need to be an essential part of this blueprint as organizational learning involves all the individuals in the organization.

The broad argument for the learning organization is that:

- we are now in a world of global information- and technology-driven organizations;

- success will depend on the speed with which new information or intelligence is communicated and applied to current operations, problems and opportunities;

- storage, transfer and retrieval of this new information is essentially technology-driven, but application of that information is people-driven and will be heavily dependent on the strength of conversations, relationships and personal, social and professional networks;

- applying the new information effectively means that people – and organizations – will need to learn to do things differently and quickly;

- since new information is becoming continuously available, learning will need to be continuous both for individuals and for organizations.

It therefore follows that only individuals and organizations that actively manage their learning processes will be successful – or, indeed, will survive and thrive!

WHAT IS A LEARNING ORGANIZATION?

In *The Power of Learning*, Mayo and Lank (1994) offer the following definition: 'A learning organization harnesses the full brain power, knowledge and experience available to it, in order to evolve continually for the benefit of all its stakeholders.'

This evolution of learning is fundamental to development, for as Reg Revans (in Pedler, 2008) explains: 'Development depends on learning agility and learning needing to be equal to or greater than the rate of change.' A more in-depth perspective is offered by Senge (1992), who notes:

> Most of us, at one time or another, have been part of a great 'team', or group of people who functioned together in an extraordinary way – who trusted each other, who complemented each other's strengths and weaknesses and compensated for each other's limitations, who had common goals that were larger than individual goals and who produced extraordinary results. I have met many people who have experienced this sort of profound teamwork – in sports or in the performing arts or in business. Many say they have spent much

of their life looking for that experience again. What they experienced was a learning organization.

Senge, author of *The Fifth Discipline* and credited as one of the main architects of the concept of the learning organization, points out that the unit of the small team or small business may be the best way to recognize how the learning organization works in practice. Successful large organizations may, of course, comprise a large number of small teams working coherently together towards a shared vision and common goals.

Senge's focus on the team in the world of sport and the performing arts also helps to highlight the potential role of the coach and mentor within a learning organization. As we have already mentioned, successful sporting and performing arts teams have long been associated with the high profile given to their coaches and mentors.

Constraints and contradictions

However, there are other powerful forces that are changing both the way organizations are structured and the way that they will increasingly behave. In most organizations there is constant pressure to reduce costs and maximize profits, or give greater value for money for the services they provide. This has led to a widespread short-term focus on immediate results and constant efforts to reduce the numbers of people employed in organizations.

Flatter management structures, process re-engineering and excellent customer service initiatives are resulting in greatly increased pressures on people. It has also meant an end to the idea that people will have a job for life or a single career that is actively managed and developed for them by the organization for which they work. People are having to become more responsible for managing their own careers and for continuous learning of new knowledge and skills if they are to remain 'employable'.

There is clearly a potential conflict between the need for organizations to actively structure and manage the learning potential of their people and the pressures to change the nature of employment contracts towards a short-term 'only as we need you' basis. New attitudes and new techniques will have to develop to reconcile these conflicts. As Handy comments in *The Age of Unreason* (2002) this is changing people's psychological contract with their employers and the need for individuals to both create and manage their portfolio career.

Mayo and Lank (1994) suggest that these new philosophies and practices will be reflected in the development of new attitudes by 'model' employees of the learning organization. They express their view in the following credo:

▌ As an individual, I do not expect the organization primarily to manage my career or my learning.

▌ I acknowledge that it is in my interest to enhance my personal value and to look after both my internal and my external continuing employability.

▌ I need a lot of support from my manager, who can allocate funds to me, empower me to manage my time between learning experiences and work achievements, and can be a coach to me in passing on his or her own experiences or help me through certain job-related experiences.

▌ I need the support of the organization as well.

▌ I want to be recognized for my increased value through learning.

▌ Both my manager and I can benefit from expertise in the management of learning from a specialist; and I need to be able to tap into databases of learning opportunities relevant to the organization I work in to enable me to make good choices.

Resistance to change

The speed at which these kinds of attitudes, expectations and practices may develop is clearly debatable. The extent of the changes required should not be underestimated. In Britain, the culture of management and leadership is still tainted with the Taylorist principles of 'command and control' and this is compounded by a culture of learning still dominated by the traditional 'chalk and talk' method of delivery.

Despite the introduction of student loans, students' learning is often perceived as being provided by the state 'free of charge' until they are in their early 20s. This has then followed in the world of work, where the employer was seen to have taken on the responsibility for training individuals and indeed for the management of their career.

These attitudes combine to produce a powerful cocktail of resistance to change.

Transformation and acceptance of the very different attitudes, practices and structures required of a learning organization full of people open, willing and ready to learn will not be easy. Only those organizations that actively want to do so will make progress. The easy option for many currently successful organizations will be to remain passive or simply pay lip-service to change while profits continue to be made today. However, success, even in the short term, it is argued, will only come to those who systematically tackle the new challenges posed by advocates of the learning organization.

TOWARDS A LEARNING ORGANIZATION MODEL

Psychologist and author Graham Guest has written extensively in various publications on this subject and advocates the importance of understanding how mental models can help us to understand complex new ideas and to bring alive the concept of the learning organization. Discussing Senge's ideas, he writes (Guest, 1999):

- Mental models are deeply ingrained assumptions by which we make sense of the world. In a learning organization these models will always be challenged to discover whether they are the best representations of exactly what is happening at any one time.

- Personal mastery is the discipline of continually clarifying and deepening personal vision; it represents the learning organization's spiritual foundation.

- Team learning starts with dialogue, which in turn involves learning how to recognize the patterns of interaction in teams.

- Building shared vision involves adopting shared pictures of the future that foster genuine commitment rather than merely compliance.

- Systems thinking, Senge's fifth discipline, sees beyond isolated events into deeper patterns and connections; whereas event thinking is linear, systems thinking is cyclical, relying on constant feedback.

To these five disciplines, Guest suggests adding the three complementary processes of:

1. coaching;

2. mentoring; and

3. effective benchmarking.

A learning organization could therefore be represented as in Figure 4.1.

Figure 4.1 A model of 'the learning organization'

The new agenda for the learning organization

The concept of the learning organization produces an agenda for all types of organizations that includes:

▌ an increased focus on learning and development as the critical means of ensuring organizational effectiveness and sustainable competitive advantage;

▌ encouraging as many people as possible, and certainly all managers, to become coaches to ensure learning occurs in the workplace and elsewhere;

▌ establishing mentoring programmes to help to support learning (sometimes these will involve specially trained coach-mentors);

▌ identifying the key personal skills necessary for individuals to operate successfully in a learning organization as well as their life in general.

In a learning organization, people will be regularly encouraged to accept the continual need to move from their current standards of performance to higher levels and to see that continuous learning is the key to continuous improvements in performance. It is an essential role of the coach-mentor to help to maintain the focus on learning opportunities and benefits.

Therefore it will come as no surprise that we offer the following definition of the overall aim of coaching and mentoring within the learning organization:

> The aim is to help and support people to manage their own learning in order that they may develop their skills, improve their performance, maximize their potential, and enable them to become the person they want to be.

This is supported by Caplin (2003) who says: 'Learning is the only unique resource which we have.'

CHOOSING HOW BEST TO LEARN

Only a few lucky people find learning easy. One of the main reasons is that most of us are used to being taught in much the same way. Yet we know that, given the chance, we prefer to choose to work in ways that suit us best. Learning is both highly personal and individualistic. So, to make learning 'easier', why not help people choose to learn in ways that suit them best? To do this, the coach-mentor needs to appreciate at least the basics of what we now understand about the way that people learn. They might well start by examining their own approaches and preferences.

From a range of publications we are aware that there is some fascinating research being done on the power and potential of the brain's design for human learning, development and growth – how we think through all of our nerve nets: with our brain and our heads;

with our emotions and feelings; and with our spirits to make sense and meaning of our experiences. There is also a developing appreciation of how the brain has a huge untapped capacity to grow and develop new neural pathways throughout our lives, which develops our intelligences, enables us to learn, unlearn and relearn, and which consequently enables us to change our perceptions, perspectives and behaviours. As Lucas (2001) says: 'The brain loves to explore and make sense of the world; likes to make connections; thrives on patterns; loves to imitate and does not perform well under too much stress.'

There is a great deal of research available on how adults learn best. It is often suggested that there are three key questions you need to be able to answer before beginning to understand what approach might suit you:

1. How do you perceive information most easily: do you learn best by seeing, hearing, moving or touching?

2. How do you organize and process the information you receive: are you predominantly left brain, right brain, analytical or global?

3. What conditions are necessary to help you to take in and store the information you are learning: are they emotional, social, physical and environmental factors?

It is now widely accepted that, for deep learning to take place, it is preferable for people to use several intelligences working together and supporting each other. Intelligence is now often considered in three main areas:

1. IQ (Intelligence Quotient) – focuses on the linear, logical and rational.

2. EQ (Emotional Intelligence) – focuses on our self-awareness and management of self in relation to others and the environment.

3. SQ (Spiritual intelligence) – focuses on our searches for meaning, integration and authenticity.

Other writers, such as Gardner (2006), emphasize that in fact there are multiple intelligences and people apply their 'learning intelligences' in many different ways, such as their ability to:

▌ speak and write well;

▌ reason, calculate and handle logical thinking;

▌ paint, take great photographs or create sculpture;

▌ use their hands or body;

▌ compose songs, sing or play musical instruments;

▌ relate to others;

▌ access their inner feelings.

Emotional intelligence

> An emotional content to learning is inevitable, because learning begins in that part of the brain.

As we have discovered more about the way the brain works, the more it has become clear that there is an important connection between learning and our emotions. As Maddern (1994) explains in *Accelerated Learning*: 'Emotional intelligence, it is claimed, is a far more accurate indicator of future success than the historical attachment to measuring IQ and classroom-based learning success.' The theory of EQ has been credited to the US academics John D Mayer and Peter Salovey, who define emotional intelligence as: 'The ability to perceive, to integrate, to understand and reflectively manage one's own and other people's feelings' (Salovey *et al*, 2004).

Science journalist Daniel Goleman is currently the best-known writer on the subject. Goleman's contribution to the EQ arena has been to translate the wealth of academic research on the subject into language that the non-academic can understand. He has therefore given credibility to the case for new and more sophisticated learning methodologies that practitioners have long understood but have, until recently, failed to convince the policy makers to accept.

The insights gained from emotional intelligence, it is claimed, help to explain why the traditional predominance of classroom-based education and training has so often failed so many people. Put simply, it is now possible to show scientifically why learning knowledge about facts, learning technical skills and learning personal skills each involves different parts of the brain and thus requires different approaches and especially different time dimensions.

Our spiritual intelligence

In recent years there has been increasing interest in spiritual intelligence (SQ), or what some people are calling the 'ultimate intelligence'.

Zohar and Marshall (2001) have written well and extensively on this. They say SQ is the intelligence with which we balance meaning and value and use to place our lives in a wider context. They go on to suggest that SQ is the ultimate intelligence in that it integrates all our intelligences, for without it both EQ and IQ cannot function and will crumble away.

Advances in science have given us permission to pay attention to, value and process information and learning that we are absorbing not only from our minds, but from also our hearts, gut and body. It is beginning to be recognized that we learn through our body's systems: with our brain and with our heads, with our emotions and our feelings, and with our spirits to derive meaning from our experiences. As Rogers (in Lucas, 2001) explains: 'Significant learning combines the logical and intuitive, the intellect and the feelings, the concept and the experience, the idea and the meaning.'

Our learning preferences

Clearly, there are a number of variables to consider when you begin to think about how you might learn more easily. Considering learning as a process offers some valuable practical insights.

Learning can be described as the process of acquiring new knowledge, understanding, skills and/or wisdom. It is also believed to be a continuous cycle, and Figure 4.2 illustrates how people learn from experience. As we have all found, the process does not have a beginning, middle or an end. Depending upon the learning situation, people – and indeed organizations – can enter the cycle at any time. The most effective learning, however, will take place when you take the opportunity to complete all the stages in the cycle.

Experience   This is the actual learning experience. It may be:
  ▪ Reactive – something that happens to you, or
  ▪ Proactive – an experience that you deliberately seek out.

Reflection   A non-judgemental look back at what happened in the learning experience. This vital stage can be achieved quite quickly without seriously disrupting the work activity.

Conclusion   Drawing conclusions from the thoughts and notes made at the reflection stage to identify the lessons learnt.

Plan   Planning and testing the lessons learnt from the conclusions, so that they can be related and applied to similar situations in the future.

Figure 4.2   The learning process (based on Kolb's cycle)

The Mellander Learning Cycle (Lucas, 2001) further develops the Kolb Learning Cycle and argues that learning is built up from an iteration of:

▌ Motivation: being mentally prepared and receptive.

▌ Information: having facts and data changed into information.

▌ Processing: having information converted into experience and insight.

▌ Conclusion: having the moment of discovery as experience and insight are converted into knowledge and wisdom.

▌ Application: having knowledge converted into skills and attitudes.

▌ Feedback: experiencing further reflection and refinement.

Everyone will find some stages in this learning cycle easier than others. Your preference for a particular stage in the continuous learning cycle reflects your preferred learning style. Recognizing your own style, or combination of styles, will help you to select learning opportunities that best suit you. Equally important, learning style analysis suggests what you may have to do to adjust your preferences to make the most of the learning opportunities that are actually available. Life does not always present us with the options to do exactly what we choose.

Peter Honey and Alan Mumford are acknowledged as UK experts and influential thinkers on the topic of learning styles, although other writers have questioned some of their ideas. In their book, *Using Your Learning Styles* (1986) they identified four styles, which link with the learning cycle discussed above. They have characterized the styles as follows.

Activists (experience)

▌ Activists are open-minded rather than sceptical. This tends to make them enthusiastic about everything new.

▌ Their philosophy is 'I'll try anything once' – they tend to act first and consider the consequences later.

▌ They fill their days with activity and tackle problems by brain-storming.

People who feel that they fit this description are likely to learn best from activities where:

▌ it's appropriate to 'have a go';

▌ they can get involved in short activities such as role-plays, and where they are in the limelight;

▌ they are thrown in at the deep end;

▌ there is a lot of excitement and a range of changing tasks to tackle, usually involving people.

Reflectors (reflection)

▌ Reflectors like to stand back and consider experiences, observing them from many different perspectives and listening to others before making their own comment.

▌ The thorough collection and analysis of data about experiences and events is what counts, so they tend to postpone reaching definitive conclusions for as long as possible.

▌ When they act, it is as part of a larger picture that includes the past as well as the present and others' observations as well as their own.

People who fit this description are likely to learn best from situations where:

▌ they can stand back from events and listen and observe;

▌ they can carry out research or analysis;

▌ they can decide in their own time, and have the chance to think before acting;

▌ they have the opportunity to review what they have learnt.

Theorists (conclusion)

▌ Theorists adapt and integrate observations into complex but logically sound theories, thinking through problems in a step-by-step way.

▌ They tend to be perfectionists who are uncomfortable unless things are tidy and fit into a rational scheme.

▌ They are keen on basic assumptions, principles, theories, models and systems thinking.

People who feel they are a theorist are likely to learn best when:

▌ they are intellectually stretched, eg through being allowed to question assumptions or logic;

▮ the situation has a structure and clear purpose;

▮ they can deal with logical, rational argument, which they have time to explore;

▮ they are offered interesting concepts, although they might not be immediately relevant.

Pragmatists (plan)

▮ Pragmatists are keen on trying out theories, ideas and techniques to see if they work in practice.

▮ They positively search out new ideas and take the first opportunity to experiment.

▮ They like to get on with things and act quickly and confidently on ideas, being impatient with extensive discussion.

As a pragmatist, you are likely to learn best from situations where you can:

▮ use techniques with obvious practical benefits;

▮ implement what you have learnt immediately;

▮ try out and practise techniques;

▮ see an obvious link between the subject matter and a real problem or opportunity at work.

Many people have found Honey and Mumford's learning preference types both helpful and easy to apply (perhaps because they tend to simplify a much more complex set of explanations).

We are not suggesting that people cannot learn from situations that do not suit their preferences. However, the learning experience is enhanced if there is a blended approach between the activist, reflector, pragmatist and theorist learning experiences and where learning opportunities are taken, transferred and cross-referenced from work and home, past and present. Our experience has shown that people learn more effectively if they can:

▮ choose learning opportunities that suit their preferred learning style(s);

▌ harness their multiple intelligences;

▌ go through the whole of the learning cycle.

This makes it important for individuals to develop each of their learning styles so that they can successfully adapt their style of learning to take advantage of each stage in the cycle. Knowledge of these learning styles will help you to:

▌ recognize your preferred learning styles and those of your colleagues;

▌ design or seek out learning opportunities that will suit your preferred learning style;

▌ focus on developing your least preferred styles so that you can make the most of the learning cycle.

Learning reflects personal style and preferences. The key to optimizing learning lies in understanding your own, and your learners' learning style and preferences both in the perception and the processing of information.

Many people have found that recognizing their own style is one of the most revealing and powerful pieces of information they can obtain. It often helps to explain many earlier problems with learning and gaining qualifications and, of course, it helps to highlight the differences between colleagues and friends, both in terms of learning and also in how they prefer to work.

Learning with our head and our heart

As we have discovered more about the way the brain works, the more it has become clear that there is an important connection between learning and our emotions. It is also clear that our IQ (intellectual intelligence), EQ (emotional intelligence) and SQ (spiritual intelligence) support each other, cooperating across thinking systems to link together the logical, serial and deterministic with our creative and contextualizing intelligences. To maximize their learning, people need to hold together thinking and doing with processes of feeling and being. In other words, to think with their heads and their hearts, which might seem to cut across much of traditional Western religious, education and business models.

Taking responsibility for your own learning means learning at the level of both the head and the heart. Knowing what you think about an issue is only half of the story and, therefore, you have only learnt half of what there is to learn. Understanding how you feel about an issue is the second, and perhaps more difficult, half.

Getting into the habit of treating yourself as a whole person will enhance your learning. Regularly asking yourself, 'How do I feel about this issue?' and, more important, 'Why do I feel this way?' is a good discipline to get you started down the route of self-awareness and understanding. This is a basic building block for someone serious about learning. Making this link between thoughts, feelings and behaviour is the key to developing new insights and self-awareness which, in turn, can facilitate self-management.

The language of learning

When you are trying to understand new ideas, apply new techniques or develop new attitudes at work, it can be very confusing indeed if key terms are defined in ways that can be interpreted differently by different people. This is certainly true with terms like 'learning', 'training', 'development', 'coaching' and 'mentoring'. While it is quite reasonable for organizations to choose their own definitions to suit their own situations, the reality is often that this clarity is not provided.

Tute (1995) highlighted some of these issues:

> Training, education and development are close relations. Yet, in vital respects, training is the polar opposite of education and development. Consider first who owns the learning agenda, because that determines the effect the outcome has on the business's future.
>
> Take training: in its pure form, the learning agenda is someone else's. The direction is outside-in. Authority is top-down. Source material is an external view of best practice, whether set by national standards, a profession or trainer. The values are conformity and compliance.
>
> Compare this with education and development. The agenda is that of the learner. The direction is inside-out. Authority is bottom-up. Source material is the learner's untapped potential and the variety of values found in humankind. The values are challenge and change.
>
> Pilots learn to fly aircraft through the process of training. MBA students learn to manage the future through the process of education. The effect of training is convergence. The effect of education and development is divergence. Values, opinions, behaviour and culture are all affected. If we train MBA students and educate pilots, we are headed for a nosedive.

Julie Starr provides a definition of the role of coach-mentoring for learning in her book, *The Coaching Manual* (2003): 'Coaching is about enabling people to create change through learning. It is also about being more, doing more, achieving more, and above all contributing more.'

LEARNING OR DEVELOPMENT?

The learning 'process' shows that people learn from experiences, whether they happen accidentally or are actively sought, for example by attending a series of lectures, or using an open learning module. As a result of these learning experiences, people reflect on them – consciously or unconsciously – and therefore draw conclusions that lead them to plan to act differently next time. This, in turn, leads to a new experience and thus the cycle begins again. Indeed it is likely to be a continuous process. For learning to be optimized and sustained, the cycle must be completed.

Development, on the other hand, is the 'process' of moving from one level of performance to a new and different level. Development can be said to have occurred when a learner can demonstrate that he or she can perform consistently at the new level of performance. Development therefore implies the need for clear standards of performance and for methods of measurement or assessment against those standards.

The development process is also related to the state of mind or attitude of the performer. It is sometimes illustrated graphically, as a development cycle. The development cycle can be best described as moving from unconscious incompetence through to unconscious competence: from 'I don't know what I don't know', through 'I do know what I don't know', 'I can do it if I think about it', to 'I can do it naturally without thinking.' If we do not constantly strive to develop and start a new and higher cycle of development, there is the danger of moving into bad habits or apathy. It is then possible to become unconsciously incompetent again while we think we are still competent, because the skills have changed or we have not kept up to date. Figure 4.3 provides an illustration of this cycle.

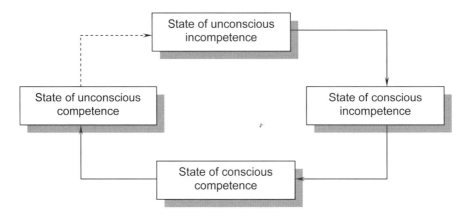

Figure 4.3 The development cycle

A popular example of this model is driving a car:

▮ Unconscious of the need for competence – at an early age, an individual may be completely unaware of the needs or techniques for driving a car.

▮ Conscious of incompetence – as they enter their teens, people become aware of the need to pass a driving test with its clear standards of both knowledge and skill.

▮ Conscious competence – after driving lessons and passing the test, people tend to drive in a very deliberate way, observing the rules and techniques they have been taught.

▮ Unconscious competence – after several years' experience of driving, people tend to do it automatically to the standards required.

However, how many of us can say we would pass the driving test now if we had to retake it? Have we kept up to date with the Highway Code? Do we know and always obey all the current regulations? Or have we become unconsciously incompetent again?

Development can clearly be seen to be a progression from one stage to another, but what drives the development process is the learning of new knowledge, understanding, skills and behaviours. This can be illustrated as in Figure 4.4

Seen in this way, it is clear that different learning needs exist and different learning techniques are required at different stages of the

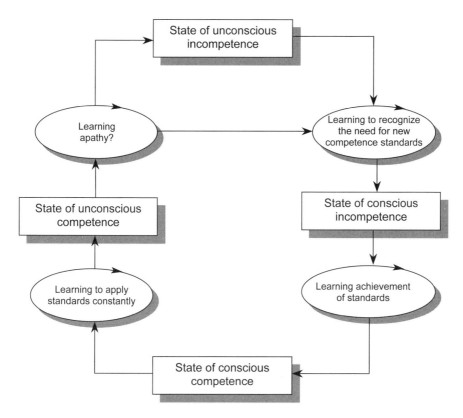

Figure 4.4 The development cycle progression

development process to drive individual performance to higher levels. It also illustrates the very real change that can occur when someone reaches a prescribed level of performance and operates with unconscious competence. Apathy and complacency can set in; this is often described as the 'comfort zone'. The task for the coach-mentor is to be able to recognize all the stages of the development process and their related learning needs and, in particular, the importance of avoiding the learning apathy or unconscious incompetence stage.

SELF-MANAGED LEARNING

These examples show that one of the key purposes of coach-mentoring is to empower the learner to take charge of his or her own learning: to become what might be called a 'self-managed learner'. The emphasis on many development programmes is to encourage learners to do the work themselves and to reflect back so the coach-mentor acts as a mirror. The discipline of the self-managed learning approach puts the onus on learners to use their coach-mentor as a sounding board but to solve their own problems. The coach- mentor's role is to ensure it is the learner's agenda that is discussed.

We believe that encouraging self-managed learning has many benefits:

▌ It encourages people to reflect on the wide range of learning opportunities available to attain goals. Getting people to think more flexibly about the opportunities that are out there, about learning, about developing themselves and about the pros and cons of where they are at the moment can be very advantageous and contribute significantly to morale.

▌ It can also improve the capacity for individuals to deal with change. When there are potential organizational changes being announced, many people find it inherently threatening. Coach-mentoring can contribute to people's comfort about change and give a greater sense of self-determination. It can also help as part of a cultural shift.

▌ It can help to address communication deficits. The process can expose a few gaps in comprehension, for example, where line managers are not making it clear to staff what is expected of them. Following such a process can help to identify where some of the basics have been neglected.

Learning inefficiencies

In his book *Effective Learning* (1999), Mumford highlights the main reasons for learning inefficiencies. We perceive these as a continuum ranging from failures of perception to failures of implementation. Our interpretation is shown in Figure 4.5.

A successful coach-mentor therefore, needs to understand the range of factors that influence a learner's perception of learning opportunities as well as the factors that influence the effective implementation of those opportunities. Motivational factors are also critical. We'll consider each of these in turn.

PERCEPTION

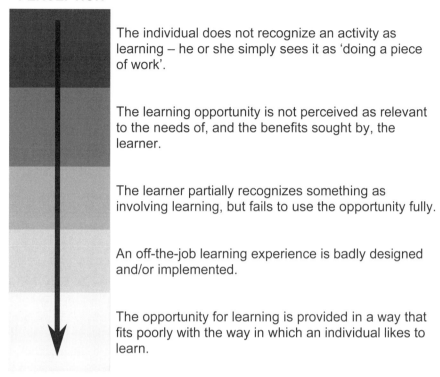

The individual does not recognize an activity as learning – he or she simply sees it as 'doing a piece of work'.

The learning opportunity is not perceived as relevant to the needs of, and the benefits sought by, the learner.

The learner partially recognizes something as involving learning, but fails to use the opportunity fully.

An off-the-job learning experience is badly designed and/or implemented.

The opportunity for learning is provided in a way that fits poorly with the way in which an individual likes to learn.

IMPLEMENTATION

Figure 4.5 A five-point scale of learning inefficiencies

Perception of opportunities

The first step in developing an accurate perception of learning opportunities is to establish that a real need to learn exists. Some people may be genuinely unaware that they need to learn anything new at all. Once a need has been recognized, however, it is likely that previous experiences of learning will significantly affect perceptions or paradigms. People who equate learning only with the classroom or training course will have a limited vision of learning and will need to be made aware of the many opportunities for learning that exist in the workplace. Past experiences of learning – particularly if they were negative – will also have a powerful influence.

As Hay (1995) explains: 'I understand paradigm shift to mean that we change to such a different model for perceiving the world that we realize that we have shifted to a different level of awareness.' It is probably true to say that most people are only vaguely aware of the learning process and are therefore quite likely to miss opportunities.

This is particularly true when it comes to recognizing the valuable opportunities to learn from mistakes. All too often, mistakes are associated with blame and denial and are quickly passed over and forgotten. The culture of the organization is important in this respect. If the prevailing culture is one of blame and fear, then the perception of learning needs and opportunities is likely to be correspondingly low. Similarly, if the structure and nature of a job is restrictive, repetitive and boring, it is more difficult to stimulate enthusiasm for on-the-job learning. Creating a genuine and active learning culture around a learner's current job is a key task of the modern coach-mentor.

Implementation of learning opportunities

Assuming a reasonably high level of awareness and perception of learning opportunities, learning effectiveness can be significantly influenced by the possibility or reality of the way the opportunities are implemented. For instance:

▎ A learner may imagine that a range of opportunities exists for him or her, but in reality these may not actually be easily available or affordable.

▎ The impact of the line manager and colleagues may also influence the implementation of opportunities. The line manager who only pays lip-service to the need for learning will often find reasons to deny access or adequate time.

▎ Operational pressures from colleagues and direct reports may also lessen a learner's willingness and ability to seize relevant opportunities.

▎ The quality of the coach, mentor, trainer or facilitator will have a powerful influence on the quality of the learning experience.

▎ Learners themselves may have blockages to learning of which they may be unaware. This is particularly true of what are called 'defensive barriers' when, for reasons of status, prestige or pride, a learner unconsciously fails to take maximum advantage of a learning opportunity.

- Blockages to learning may come from the learning methods employed. The learning design or technology used may simply be inappropriate to the content.

- The learning institution itself may be inappropriate – a college environment might be unsuitable for a programme for high-flying marketing executives, or an Outward Bound course inappropriate for learning basic financial management techniques.

- The method of assessing and evaluating performance, progress and results can also be critical. An obsession with passing a test to gain a qualification can be a block to developing a wider understanding of a subject or skill.

An awareness of these 'implementation factors' is crucial if the coach and mentor are to help to avoid learning inefficiencies.

The learner's motivation

An individual's desire to make the most of learning opportunities is often influenced by his or her perception of the rewards and punishment involved. 'The more you learn, the more you'll earn', for example, has become a recognized phrase. A person's social and career successes to date, as well as his or her future aspirations and vision, are also important motivational influences. These perceptions will clearly be different for individual people at various stages of their careers.

Our own research evidence suggests, however, that learners are motivated most effectively by the interest, enjoyment, satisfaction and challenge of the learning process itself rather than simply by the rewards and punishments related to learning. The former factors are termed 'intrinsic' motivators, the latter 'extrinsic' motivators. As we have already seen, individual learning style preferences and learning capabilities each have a bearing on a learner's motivation. Faced with opportunities that do not appeal or which seem too difficult, a learner's motivation is likely to be low.

Finally, an individual's self-confidence and general personality have to be taken into account. Building self-confidence, self-awareness and self-esteem are a critical part of the modern coach-mentor's role. The higher the levels of confidence, awareness and esteem, the higher the learner's motivation to seize learning opportunities and to take responsibility for improving his or her levels of performance will be.

The challenge for the modern coach and mentor is first to recognize the interrelated influences in the 'learning matrix' and then to identify techniques, tactics and skills to handle them. Figure 4.6 illustrates the range of influences that have to be managed by the successful coach or mentor.

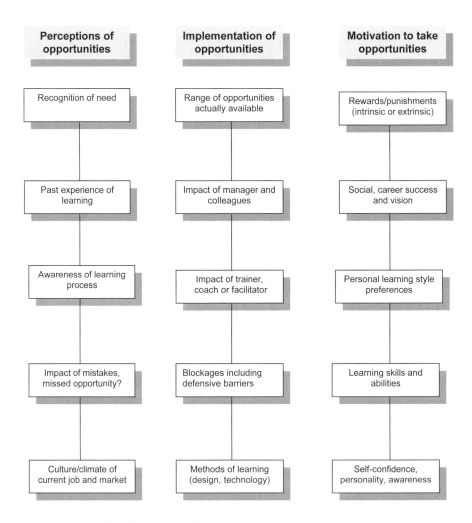

Figure 4.6   The learning efficiency matrix

Training inefficiencies

Coaching and mentoring have now become one of the most frequently used approaches in the UK corporate learning armoury, after on-the-job-training and the traditional training course. Viewing them as just another weapon in the learning mix may suit some organizations. For others, they may provide what some people describe as the 'essential glue that makes training courses stick'. What they are referring to is that coaching and mentoring programmes can provide an ongoing and one-to-one opportunity to reinforce and apply the learning that occurs in a typical classroom-based training course. As with Goleman's popularizing of emotional intelligence, so coaching and mentoring may now be the 'popular' answer to deficiencies that have long been known to exist with traditional training methodologies.

In the last century, research by the German psychologist Ebbinghaus (1850–1909) produced results (since validated by scores of other research), which showed that 90 per cent of what was learnt in a class was forgotten within 30 days and 60 per cent was forgotten after one hour. Similarly, Roy Harrison, Policy Adviser for the Institute of Personnel and Development, reported recent US research which showed that on average only 10–20 per cent of learning through training transfers into people's work (Harrison, 1998). Other surveys have shown that more than half of those attending training courses felt that 'they already knew most or quite a lot of the content', a third felt that 'the training made no difference at all to their performance' and only 2 per cent felt that 'the training had broken new ground'.

With our current level of understanding about how people learn, the main explanation for these types of deficiencies is most probably the application of the outdated approaches of delivering learning:

> People have not made a clear distinction in training methodologies between kinds of abilities, technical skills and the domain of personal abilities, that I call emotional intelligence. But the brain does… Emotional intelligence, unlike the cognitive and technical skills, entails a more primitive part of the brain – the limbic centres or the emotional brain. The emotional brain learns differently from the neo-cortex, where technical skills and cognitive abilities reside. The neo-cortex learns fine in the classroom model, or from a book or from a CD-ROM. In other words, it learns quickly, it can learn in a single trial, its mode is associational. It ties new knowledge to an existing network and that happens very quickly in the brain.
>
> The emotional brain learns in a completely different mode, through repetition, through practice, through models. In other words, it learns through a model which is that of habit change. That being the case, people need a certain set of elements in a training approach if it is going to be effective. (Goleman, 1996)

Goleman bases his criticisms of these traditional methods on what he sees as the widespread failure to appreciate the implications of emotional intelligence theories. He claims: 'It should come as no surprise then that we advocate that, for certain topics (like personal skills), coaching and mentoring could be most sensibly seen as "preferred options" in helping people to learn.'

Structured reflection

Helping people to learn how to learn is the main aim of the coach-mentor. It is clear that new approaches to learning are essential. It is also clear to us that the definition of learning merely as a process does not really suit its overall importance in our emerging society. We therefore offer the following definition: 'Learning is both a process and a continuous state of mind, which transcends all traditional organizational boundaries and structures, and has become a central feature of the way we live.'

So how does an individual increase his or her ability to learn? Lucas (2001) believes it is though studying the 5Rs: 'So, think not of the 3Rs, but of the exciting new 5Rs – Resourcefulness, Remembering, Resilience, Reflectiveness, and Responsiveness. These skills are at the heart of what makes a competent lifelong learner.'

Whitmore (1997) believes these qualities are at the core of coaching: 'Building awareness, responsibility and self-belief is the goal of a coach... our potential is realized by optimizing our own individuality and uniqueness, never by moulding them to another's opinion of what constitutes best practice.'

We believe Whitmore's goal for coaches is best achieved by concentrating on the most important of Lucas's 5Rs: 'reflectiveness or 'structured reflection'. As Warren Bennis wrote (in Lucas, 2001):

> Reflecting on experience is a means of having a Socratic dialogue with yourself, asking the right questions at the right time, in order to discover the truth of yourself and your life. What really happened? Why did it happen? What did it do to me? What did it mean to me? In this way, one locates and appropriates the knowledge one needs or, more precisely, recovers what one had forgotten, and becomes, in Goethe's phrase, the hammer rather than the anvil.

Reflection can be considered as essentially a mental process. It provides a way of thinking about relatively complex experiences or un-structured and disparate thoughts, behaviours and feelings for which there is no obvious pattern or theme, with the purpose of extracting learning and meaning.

At the Oxford School, we use a powerful tool called the 'Reflection note', which forces learners to take a structured and disciplined approach to reflecting on their experiences and on the links between thoughts, feelings and behaviour. Reflective writing provides an opportunity for coach-mentors to gain further and deeper insights from their practice through deeper reflection on their experiences, and through further consideration of other perspectives from people and theory.

When reflecting on an experience in order to learn, we would encourage you to explore the model illustrated in Figure 4.2. This corresponds to the four learning style preferences described earlier:

1. What has happened and why did it happen that way? (Activist)

2. How did you think, feel and behave? (Reflector)

3. What have you learnt from, what sense can you make from, the experience? (Theorist)

4. What are you going to do in the future as a result of this experience? (Pragmatist)

Reflection note

▨ Exactly what happened and what do you believe caused it to happen that way?

▨ How did you think, feel and behave during the experience?

▨ What were the main learning points for you from this experience?

▨ What might you do differently in the future, if anything, following this learning experience?

Reflective learning

Elaine Patterson had been a senior manager and director in the NHS and Civil Service for over 20 years when maternity leave forced a re-evaluation of her priorities, interests and commitments. Elaine had always been interested in people and people development and came to the Oxford School's coaching and mentoring qualification programmes because of the content and blended learning approach. Below are extracts from her final assessment to the School. We have included what Elaine wrote about her learning experience to illustrate the profound and transformational effects of deep learning.

The blended learning programme was completely new to me but gave me a useful range of complementary challenges and support, while also freeing me to experiment. The process felt iterative, dynamic and unfolding rather than linear.

I found the focus on holistic learning, reflection and the production of evidence of learning new but, once I broke through my initial hesitation, refreshing. I also regularly reviewed my progress against my self-assessment scores.

I enjoyed the challenge of separating out my observations of what was happening from how I behaved, thought or felt about the situation and from which I could surface my main learning and resulting action points.

As I worked through the programme and pulled from past and current work and life experiences I felt that I was continually asking myself:

▌ What am I learning about myself?
▌ What am I learning about myself as a coach-mentor?
▌ What am I learning about my learners?
▌ What am I learning about coach-mentoring in the context of my organization and work?

My learning curve felt initially very faltering and steep but then rapidly accelerated as I was able to put the parts of the jigsaw together – and felt very reminiscent of learning to ski! I felt unsure, excited but willing to discover and explore. I felt like a tanker starting to leave the dock but gradually with practice and commitment felt myself start to feel in the flow; to start to relax and open up; to trust myself to find the 'knight's move' question; to rewire based on a dialogue with experience and learning; a moving from 'doing' to 'being'.....

From this I have learnt to appreciate and accept strengths without focusing only on my gaps and areas for development. I now actively welcome and encourage feedback as well as being comfortable with providing constructive feedback. I have also learnt to ditch a misplaced and handicapping sentimentality, to be more direct in expressing myself and my needs appropriately, and to be more pragmatic.

Building 'ballast'

It was in my reading about spiritual intelligence that I had become aware that while I had a strong values system I needed to create an explicit belief system or 'ballast' to support my practice as a coach-mentor. That I needed to develop a strong calm and peaceful centre within myself and that the seeds of my exploration had been germinating for a long time triggered by changing family circumstances.

I felt that I needed some framework which would provide meaning and which would help me to organize my understanding of life's apparent paradoxes or dichotomies. I learnt from Gibran's *The Prophet* that the seeds of one also contain the seeds of the other, ie love and loss; life and death; happiness and sadness; similarity and difference; togetherness and solitude; giving and receiving; trust and betrayal; and how a person's response to these inherent fractures determines an individual's capacity and capability for joy and happiness, reconciliation and forgiveness, and empathy and understanding.

Reflecting in action

I have learnt that the quality of the relationship is happening in the conversation. I have moved into reflecting in action, which is about both being in the moment and having a helicopter view of what is happening at that moment. A major learning for me is to forget about the skills and techniques and focus on the process. When I do this I have found that a greater relaxation and the release of ego paradoxically enable me to make a better social and emotional connection with the learner. Also, I have learnt to be more aware of the range of possible blocks or obstacles which can dilute focused concentration; and to acknowledge where barriers occur and for these to be honestly addressed either with the learner, as part of my own reflective practice and/or with my supervisor.

I have also learnt how to observe objectively without judgement – feeling almost like a state of 'nothingness', 'of letting go' – and where instead judgement is replaced by an all-encompassing spirit of curiosity about what is being said and what the individual is experiencing. I now try to spot what is missing or hidden and to communicate with the conscious mind through thoughts, feelings, imagery and sounds. To relax and trust that in focusing intention, thoughts and feelings follow; to experience the other person for who they are as well as what they are saying and to spot where this is going wrong. I realize that it is possible through processes of insight, self-awareness, intentional effort, practice and emotional commitment to reconfigure the brain and change behaviours.

Changing paradigms or triple-loop learning

Standing back I am now aware that I have been through a process of triple-loop learning which surpassed my expectations, providing me with the opportunity to achieve a number of paradigm shifts.

Looking back I can see that the themes underlying my work with all of my learners ultimately revolved to some extent around their search for identity; a reframing; a challenging of assumptions about themselves and their contexts; a reconnection with their values; and a search for authenticity to some degree or another. Triple-loop learning has helped me to 'listen' to how I feel and has enabled me to make a significant move to a different plane of self-awareness, self-management and responsibility. Triple-loop learning greatly deepened my personal development during the programme – and beyond – and helped me translate this into my signature presence as a coach-mentor with my learners.

Awareness of self

My developing self-awareness grew out of the task set for me to move from my current reality at the start of the programme to the achievement of my SMART goals. For me this has hinged on the development of my emotional intelligence – ie in how I manage myself and my relationships with others – together with my spiritual intelligence – ie my creative, integrative, meaning-giving and transformative centre. This with reflective practice has enabled me to move into self-coaching.

I realize that a new perception of self has emerged where my journey has taken me from director to coach-mentor; from being office-based to working from home; to working on a process rather than a content agenda; from employee to freelancer; from a DINKY (double income no kids) to a networked Mum with a range of work and leisure activities including voluntary, community and school work; from doing to being.

I am now building my life in line with my values, beliefs and way that I want to live.

'In the moment'

The work on myself has enabled me move from textbook to 'in the moment' coaching. My improved self-awareness and management of myself has enable me to manage my own reactivity when I enter the 'coaching bubble' in order to better focus totally on the learner's needs, to instinctively build empathy and rapport, to listen attentively, to ask the incisive question, to give constructive feedback, to demonstrate integrity, and to create openness and trust with positive intention.

PRINCIPLES OF ADULT LEARNING

Summing up the key principles from this chapter, we believe the main purpose of coaching and mentoring is to help the learner to learn. This is best achieved by the following.

Learning as dependent on an emotional readiness

Learning starts with an emotional readiness, a 'Get ready, go and steady', and is the relationship between the learner's interior and exterior world. Learning requires the creation of a supportive learning environment and a learner's determination and motivation to act.

Learning cannot take place without a secure base and working with the right blend of competence, support and challenge tailored for each individual learner. Fear, threat, and anxiety physically and chemically shut down the brain's capacity to learn, reducing awareness, inhibiting calculated risk-taking and forcing fight or flight.

Where coach mentoring is taking learners on an intellectual and emotional journey from current reality to their goal, the key to success lies in providing a psychological safety, a sense of time and space without fear of failure blended with challenges that do not scare but build self-esteem and self-belief. Learning has to be fun and enjoyable with a focus on what excites, enthuses, draws and inspires.

Learning starts with developing the learner's self-awareness

Learning starts with the learner's developing awareness: both in knowing what is happening and knowing what is being experienced. Awareness is built with focused attention, clarity and concentration – and is dependent on good quality feedback. It is what we are not aware of that controls us. Therefore the skill of the coach-mentor is to raise and sustain the level of awareness to the appropriate level within the goals and context of each learner.

Learning with purpose

To be effective, learning has to have a clear purpose. People need to know why they need to learn something and need to be involved in the planning and evaluation of their learning. In coaching and mentoring, the purpose of learning is almost always to achieve some kind of change. This may be to embrace a positive change or to cope appropriately with a negative change. It is the process that drives the development of increased knowledge, increased self-awareness, increased emotional and spiritual intelligence as well as increased skills and abilities.

Learning comes from experience

Adults need to learn experientially and will draw upon their reservoir of experience (including mistakes) for learning. Structured reflection helps the individual to focus and so extract the maximum effective learning from his or her experiences. The role of the coach-mentor is to suggest a motivation and a structure to improve the learner's reflection skills.

Learning as a lifelong journey

Learning has no end point and is never finished – moving instead to different levels of performance, understanding and awareness. Coach-mentors should strive to make their clients independent, self-aware and self-developing learners. Coach-mentors need to be careful not to build any dependence into the coach-mentoring relationship.

5

Awareness of individual differences

This is a completely new chapter we have added in recognition of the significant growth in interest across the coaching and mentoring profession in philosophy, psychology and human nature. One of the key functions of coaching and mentoring is to enhance self–awareness. It is our contention that if coach-mentors are unaware of their own make-up (of who they are, of their own motivations), then they are unlikely to be capable of fully understanding and helping the person they are coaching.

Each learner and each coach-mentor is different and these many differences make each of us unique. It follows then that each coach-mentoring relationship is also unique. When we think of individual differences, we typically refer to personality traits, values, beliefs, interests, intelligence, ability, personal motivation, learning styles and self-concept, race, religion and gender, to name just a few. Therefore, the best coach-mentoring interventions should be designed to identify and accommodate these personal differences and individual needs. As such, it is important that coach-mentors understand more clearly how and why people behave as they do. This brings us into the realms of psychology, psychotherapy and philosophy. These are well-established disciplines with a wide variety of theories and often strongly held differences of interpretation and opinions.

It is our view that it is not necessary to be fully qualified in these disciplines to be an effective coach-mentor but it is important to have a reasonable grounding in some of the more widely agreed aspects of these disciplines. Also it is not uncommon for sophisticated purchasers of coaching and mentoring services to ask providers to explain their particular approach. These client requirements may challenge some coach-mentors to articulate their theories about personal development, psychological models and approaches. In this chapter then, we discuss those aspects that we believe are of importance to a coach-mentor as an introduction for those who may wish to probe more deeply.

BELIEFS AND VALUES

If you believe you can or you believe you can't you are probably right. (Henry Ford)

Beliefs are those things that a person holds to be absolutely true. An individual may have thousands of beliefs: many of them adopted at early stages of his or her life from other people who were significant at that time. Even though a person's beliefs are driven by his or her values, they are important in their own right because they help shape behaviour and how events are interpreted. Some beliefs are empowering and useful to have, but there are also those that are limiting. Most people have a belief or point of view about human potential, from, 'I can do anything' through to the other end of the spectrum: 'I am the way I am and cannot change.'

The coach-mentor comes into the relationship with his or her own thoughts, opinions and judgments of the learner. A part of managing oneself while coaching is to be able to identify one's own stuff and deal with it appropriately. Coach-mentors need to understand themselves as a coach before they can hope to understand what might be going on with the learners. So if the coach-mentor can establish the learners' values, it may help them to make fulfilling choices, take appropriate decisions, formulate action plans, and lead a balanced life. Asking questions that relate to values and beliefs can help to raise the learners' self-awareness of how their feelings and behaviours are affected by actions and events that support or challenge their values. The following questions are examples a coach-mentor might use in a conversation to achieve this:

▌ Can you describe the values that drive you?

▌ Which are those things that are really important to you?

▌ How could you harness those values to help your own fulfilment and the wellbeing of those around you?

▌ What do you think are your strengths?

▌ Do you know what is at the main source of your energy and enthusiasm?

CULTURE AND DIVERSITY

A culture can provide specific ways to see the world and is influenced by many things. For a nation, these influences will include their history, geography, ethnicity and politics. For an organization, culture will be shaped by the founders, leadership, working conditions and competitors, among others. These cultural influences will be a part of the background of the learner who, it can be seen, may well belong to several cultural groups, and the coach needs to take this into account. In his book *Coaching across Cultures* (2004), Rosinski provides some useful insights and frameworks to help a coach take a multicultural approach to his or her practice and is well worth reading if you wish to broaden your understanding of this area.

Coaching is, by its very nature, a one-to-one process where personal traits and characteristics come to the fore. Therefore, a coach-mentor needs to take into account other aspects of diversity as well as culture. These include: ethnicity, religion, age, sexual orientation, physical and mental disability and gender, the latter of which is explored in more detail in the next section. However, if coach-mentors are not attuned to their own cultural and diversity issues there is a risk this may influence their coaching. Indeed, ignoring these differences in coaching for the sake of being politically correct, or because of our own discomfort, can block learning for both the coach-mentor and the learner.

Coach-mentors can also be at risk of assuming a similarity in cultures that may block the learning for their learners. It is wise to follow the advice of Adler (2002), a writer on cross-cultural issues, when she says: 'Assume difference until similarity is proven.' Often there are different ways of achieving the same common understanding. The coach-mentor should try to sensitively help the learner find alternate approaches that will work sympathetically within the specific culture or diversity while retaining the learner's own identity.

GENDER

Many coach-mentors believe that coaching men and women requires a different approach. The dynamics of gender difference have been discussed in many books: Tannen and Grey are notable authors in this field, while Thomson *et al* (2005) have related gender to the subject of leadership. They offer the following observation:

> In our view men and women lead differently; for historical reasons, business organizations bear the imprints of masculine values, norms and patterns of behaviour and that, as a result of this, the cultures of companies frequently don't 'fit' women, particularly at senior levels where women remain thin on the ground... A new compact between the sexes must be reached about how our large companies are organized, managed and led, that makes them better adapted to and more welcoming for women.

SKAI Associates' recent research (2007) in the UK makes a similar observation:

> Given that most organizations are more male dominated it's useful to ask the question, 'What would the female traits, if nurtured, bring to the organization?' Successful coaching will... find ways to have a woman's natural traits and abilities deployed at scale in the workplace. Would it be a legitimate objective for coaching in organizations to reduce the domination of traditional 'male' traits and increase the influence of 'feminine' traits?

If it is acknowledged that men and women have different traits, then SKAI Associates suggest the implications for coaching might be understood as laid out in Table 5.1

Table 5.1 Possible coaching intervention

	Things learners will stretch themselves with	Things that limit learners' potential
Men	• Being a lead – taking on the mantle of making and implementing decisions • Solving gritty problems	• Disregard relationships • Don't like/can't be bothered with collaborating • Too much operational interfering
Women	• Creative effective relationships • Working with personal independent freedom • Expressing themselves well/ being open	• Talk down personal ability – to self and others • Tend to think small(er) • Dislike confrontation

These are important issues that we recommend everyone should reflect on because it is not immediately obvious to us that it is appropriate for a coach-mentor to treat male learners differently to female learners. We believe it would be better to treat each learner as an individual and not stereotyped by gender.

PHILOSOPHIES

As we have shown in the previous chapters, you don't need to be a psychologist to know that learners' motivations are a key factor in their successful learning and effective change. As the cliché says: 'You can lead a horse to water, but you cannot make it drink.' Even when people are motivated to change, it can be all too easy for them to slip back into their old habits or resign themselves to a situation because it is part of their personality or the way they see the world.

Another way of saying 'the way they see the world' is to describe it as a personal philosophy. We believe that philosophy can be defined more fully. In our own words: 'Philosophy is the examination of basic concepts such as truth, existence, reality, causality and freedom. The combination of these basic concepts forms a person's guiding or underlying principles.'

There are many published philosophies; some more accepted and/or well known than others. There used to be a clearly defined demarcation between what were collectively know as 'Western' and 'Eastern' philosophies, but these now appear to be coming together, with the recognition that both have value. There are also a number of theories of human nature that seek to make sense of the similarities and differences between people. Many of the ideas developed by the historical and modern personality theorists stem from the basic philosophical assumptions they hold.

The following seven categories describe some of the fundamental questions that are at the root of most philosophies:

1. Hereditary versus environment – is personality largely determined by genetics/heredity (nature) or by environment and experiences (nurture), or both?

2. Freedom versus determinism – do we have control over our own behaviour; can we direct our own actions, and understand the motives behind it or is our behaviour basically determined by some other force over which we may not have control?

3. Uniqueness versus universality – are we all unique or are large groups of humans basically similar in their nature?

4. Proactive versus reactive – do we primarily act through our own initiative, or do we react to outside stimuli?

5. Optimistic versus pessimistic – are we basically positive or negative? Can we alter our personalities or do they remain the same throughout our whole lives?

6. Past versus present – is our personality created and set by early events in our lives, or can we develop our personality in response to current experiences?

7. Equilibrium versus growth – are we motivated simply to maintain a psychological balance, or are we driven by an urge to grow and develop?

You might like to take a few moments to consider and answer these questions for yourself to help to describe your own philosophy. To assist you, we have provided a framework listing the seven philosophical questions in Figure 5.1. Consider each one in turn and mark the relative point on each line to represent your own philosophical perspective.

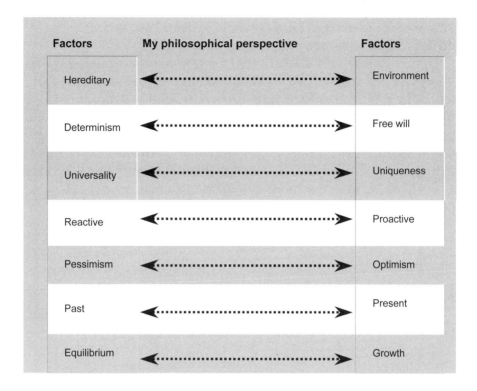

Factors	My philosophical perspective	Factors
Hereditary	◄·····················►	Environment
Determinism	◄·····················►	Free will
Universality	◄·····················►	Uniqueness
Reactive	◄·····················►	Proactive
Pessimism	◄·····················►	Optimism
Past	◄·····················►	Present
Equilibrium	◄·····················►	Growth

Figure 5.1 Philosophical perspectives

Existential philosophy

One philosophy that we believe is particularly appropriate and relevant to coaching is existentialism. This is a fusion of philosophical and psychological thought mainly founded by Soren Kierkegaard (1813–55). Existentialism, broadly defined, is a set of philosophical systems concerned with free will, choice and personal responsibility: because we make choices based on our experiences, beliefs and biases, those choices are unique to us. The key concepts are that:

▍ everyone has free will;

▍ life is a series of choices that creates stress;

▍ few decisions are without any negative consequences;

▍ some things are irrational or absurd without explanation;

▍ if one makes a decision, one must follow through.

This leads us to the well known phrase by Jean-Paul Sartre (1943): 'We do not choose to be free. We are condemned to freedom.'

The existential view holds that people have no inherent characteristics and instead are endlessly remaking or discovering themselves in a movement towards self-realization – a progression of discovering who the real 'you' is. Anxiety comes from pretending to be 'a character' by identifying ourselves with our roles, refusing to take responsibility for our choices, and taking our social attributes as 'wired in' rather than chosen. Crisis is inevitable and to be welcomed as positive because, existentialists believe, a crisis only occurs when you are equipped and ready to deal with it.

The main implications of existential philosophy for coaching are:

▧ The emphasis on 'being' rather than 'doing'.

▧ The recognition that we cannot always resolve conflict but must learn to accept and live with it.

▧ We should face uncertainty – acknowledge that change is constant – and strive to keep a balance.

Typical existential coaching questions would include:

▧ Do you like the direction of your life? If not, what are you doing about it?

▧ What are the aspects of your life that satisfy you most?

▧ What is preventing you from doing what you really want to do?

Ontological coaching

In the latter part of the 20th century, the integration of significant developments in the fields of philosophy and biology produced a new discipline with the general name of 'ontology of the human observer'. As a discipline it is grounded in recent developments in existential philosophy, the philosophy of language and the biology of cognition.

Ontology is the study of being and is an inquiry into the nature of human existence. It encompasses major existential issues of meaning, fulfilment, happiness and worthiness in our personal and professional lives. The concept is built around two key questions: what is it to be a human being, and what does it mean to live and work well? Ontological coaching focuses on exploring a person's 'way of being', referring to how they are at any point in time, and in particular refers to how they observe or perceive the world. The way of being is a dynamic interrelationship between language, emotions and physiology. Ontologists believe that:

▌ Humans are continually speaking and listening. The conversations that we participate in and the actual words we choose to use, internally and externally, form an important part of what is real for us.

▌ Humans are also emotional beings: their moods and emotions colour how they see the world and how they behave.

▌ Human physiology is the combination of the physical body, our posture, the working of our internal systems and organs.

▌ Change happens only when there are shifts in all three domains, and when this occurs a different world is observed and new possibilities for action become available to the learner.

An ontological coach-mentor seeks to facilitate learning and change by working on a combination of all three areas of the learner's language, emotions and physiology. Working on all three dimensions can not only lead to effective behavioural action, but also help to build a more meaningful life. James Flaherty is a well-known author who coaches from a principle-shaped ontological stance. He suggests that coaching should follow these five operating principles (Flaherty, 1999, pp. 10–12):

1. The relationship is the most important principle and forms the background to the coaching efforts. To be mutually satisfying the relationship must be based on mutual respect, trust and freedom of expression.

2. The coach-mentor should be pragmatic in being willing to continually learn from experience, innovate and correct what is not producing the desired practical outcome.

3. A 'two track' approach requires the coach-mentor to divide themselves into two people: the one who acts in life and the one who watches (the observer). The coach-mentor should observe

themselves and question their own assumptions and guard against their own blindness, prejudices and stubbornness.

4. The coach-mentor should acknowledge the learner is always/ already in the middle of their lives. They will already have their own way of doing things and the coach-mentor must adapt their approach to fit the learner.

5. Using only techniques doesn't work. Techniques can prevent the coach-mentor from engaging fully with the learner with openness, courage and curiosity. Techniques cannot replace the human heart and creativity in coaching.

PSYCHOLOGICAL INFLUENCES

The various branches of psychology attempt to explain how and why humans behave as they do, based on different philosophical standpoints. These psychological concepts bring with them a host of theories and models that explain the coaching and mentoring relationship.

From works such as those by the psychologist Peltier (2002) we see that a good range of psychological therapeutic frameworks are being adapted for application in the coaching context. As we have already emphasized, to practise as a coach-mentor a degree in psychology is not necessary but we do believe it is important to have a reasonable fluency in the language of psychology and a level of general understanding of the main concepts.

There are three principle psychological schools or origins: psycho-analytical, behavioural and humanistic. Each of these is sub-divided into more specialized concepts. In this section we briefly explore some of the most widely used theoretical influences that inform the coach-mentors' approach to their practice. Most relate to an existential philosophical perspective.

Humanistic

Viewing human nature as conscious, self-directed, self-actualizing and healthy distinguishes the humanistic psychology from psychoanalytic and behaviouristic psychology. Although there is no single accepted theory of what humanistic psychology actually is, there are some very consistent themes running throughout the concept. The major theme is that of change: the process of change; how humans strive for change to become more fulfilled and achieve their potential. Leading psychologists in the development of humanistic psychology were Abraham Maslow (1908–70) and Carl Rogers (1902–87). Humanistic theories emphasize:

- Growth and fulfilment of the self: through self–mastery, self-examination and self-expression.

- Our purpose in life is to progress on a continuum of development – one that starts in early childhood but often gets blocked later on in life.

- The optimistic belief that all humans are naturally good and trustworthy.

The core implications for this approach are:

- The learners know best.
- They know what is wrong.
- They know how to move forward.

Coach-mentors using a humanistic person-centred approach need to:

- Be genuine or congruent in themselves – be transparent about their motivations and have a high level of self-awareness.

- Have unconditional positive regard or non-possessive warmth – respect and accept the learner.

- Have empathetic understanding of learners – their perceptions and the ability, to stay with their emotions.

- See quality listening as an effective route to in-depth understanding.

Cognitive behavioural

Cognitive behavioural therapy (CBT) comes from a behavioural origin rather than humanistic. Its essential concept is that how people interpret an event or situation affects the way they feel about that situation and how they behave: ie it is not the situation itself that creates emotions, but rather how a person interprets that situation. This naturally leads on to the notion that if you change the way a person thinks, this will change the way a person feels and acts. Thus the route to emotional change, it is argued, is through cognitive and behaviour change.

CBT does not offer any quick fixes to achieve personal change or 'magic away' personal difficulties. Instead it emphasizes that sustained effort and commitment are required for a successful outcome to your life challenges.

CB coaching is based on a collaborative relationship that helps individuals to focus on problem solving in a structured and systematic way. Using a Socratic and non-directive approach encourages individuals to 'pull out' from themselves problem-solving strategies rather than have them handed over by the coach-mentor. CB coaching is characterized by:

▌ An emphasis on the achievement of clear short-term goals.

▌ Drawing on and adding to their existing skills helps individuals to build greater self-reliance and confidence in managing change in their lives.

▌ The ultimate goal is for the individual to become his or her own coach-mentor.

Transpersonal psychology

The *Journal of Transpersonal Psychology* describes transpersonal psychology as 'the study of humanity's highest potential, and with the recognition, understanding, and realization of intuitive, spiritual, and transcendent states of consciousness'.

Transpersonal psychology embraces a range of values such as altruism, humanitarianism, aesthetics and ethics. It is about helping an individual identify a deeper purpose, realize his or her full potential, as well as serving the wider needs of the organization and of society. This approach also emphasizes the spiritual dimension to a person's functioning, which is called the 'higher' or 'transpersonal self' and is seen as a source of wisdom and energy. It is this reference to energy, combined with values, which is most relevant in understanding the role of transpersonal coaching and how it chimes perfectly with the perception of coaching as a positive, as opposed to remedial, activity. As Whitmore (1997) says: 'If we look for where the positive energy is, the vitality, and the spirit, and explore and build on it, then this is what will grow within an individual or a company.' In turn, this will lead to transpersonal coaching being 'an empowering process'. According to Whitmore this is because: 'drilling into an individual's core values allows the coach to unearth the coachee's core strengths and creativity'.

Transpersonal coaching goes beyond the person by taking a systems approach, encouraging individuals to see themselves as part of a team, organization, family and community. A transpersonal approach to coaching would include:

- Focusing on the quality of the relationship rather than tools or techniques.

- Trusting the coaching process and respecting your intuition.

- Looking beyond the presented situation for its deeper meaning and wider implications.

- Seeing the individual as part of a complex system.

Positive psychology

Positive psychology is a relatively young branch of psychology, with Martin Seligman as its best known advocate. He has criticized other psychologies as primarily dedicated to addressing mental illness rather than mental 'wellness'. He states in his book *Learned Optimism* (2005) that: 'The keystone of high achievement and happiness is exercising your strengths.'

Therapists, counsellors, coaches, and various other psychological professionals now use these new methods and techniques to build and broaden the lives of individuals who are not necessarily suffering from mental illness or disorder. Practical applications of positive psychology include helping individuals and organizations correctly identify their strengths and use them to increase and sustain their respective levels of wellbeing.

The positive psychology concept when applied to the world of work says that a great organization must not only accommodate the fact that each employee is different, but also capitalize on these differences. It must identify each employee's natural strengths and talents and then develop them so that his or her strengths can be used for the benefit of the individual and the organization.

Questions a coach-mentor may ask when using a positive psychology approach include:

▮ What are the things that you do best?

▮ How do you know when you are at your best?

▮ Tell me about a time when you were successful at doing this before.

A potential drawback of this approach is the prevailing ethos adopted by many managers and the mindset adopted by many employees: namely, that you should tackle the person's weaknesses and the strengths will take care of themselves. However, there is a growing body of evidence that suggests the opposite. The area of potentially greatest growth is in the individual's greatest strengths. Focusing on weaknesses demotivates, resulting in reduced strengths, and does not significantly improve weaknesses.

Solutions-focused coaching

This approach moves away from problem analysis but does not ignore the problem's existence. The focus is on finding the best solution based on existing strengths and looking at what already works. A solutions focus has similar approaches to positive psychology and appreciative inquiry. All three approaches advocate a move away from focusing on the problem and recommend looking to the positives for solutions. The basic assumption of solutions-focused coaching is that for each learner specific individualized solutions for problems work best and that any person is competent to solve his or her own problems.

The structure of a solutions-focused approach might look like this:

1. Acknowledge problems.

2. Define the preferred future or solution.

3. Identify potential solutions or positive actions to achieve the solution.

4. Amplify, refine and prioritize the solutions to achieve the desired result.

Gestalt psychology

Gestalt is best known as a therapeutic approach originated by Fritz Perls (1893–1970). In this concept each person is regarded as an exploring, adapting, self-reflecting, interacting social and physical being in a process of continuous change. The person is seen holistic-ally and as an open system because existence calls for versatility and for 'creative adjustment'.

The life of each individual is full of numerous gestalts: temporary models, shapes or patterns of a person's experience that form and, when completed, dissolve. This pattern is referred to the 'cycle of experience' and problems occur when the cycle is not completed or is blocked for some reason.

The Gestalt approach has four key concepts:

1. Greater awareness of the body, the emotions, the thoughts, the self and the environment is seen as a goal in itself.

2. Focus on the here and now and personal experiments. Don't just think about it – experience it and feel it.

3. Take personal responsibility for whatever you are experiencing or doing. Don't blame the situation or other people.

4. Unfinished business or avoidance, unexpressed emotions and avoiding confrontation prevent you being fully alive.

'The paradoxical theory of change' (Biesser, 1971) is a gestalt idea that suggests that change does not occur by trying to be what you are not but, by fully embracing who you are, change happens only when you are truly yourself. Lasting change cannot be attained through coercion or persuasion.

Applying the principles of gestalt to the practice of coaching would include:

▮   The coach-mentor is part of the process; the method cannot be separated from the person.

▮ Focus on what is happening now, not solely on what is being discussed.

▮ The coach-mentor works with what is, not what should be, could be or must be.

▮ Resistance is seen as positive and healthy, to be worked with rather than against.

▮ Work with the here and now, notice where the energy is and go with it.

Transactional analysis

Transactional Analysis (TA) was developed by Eric Berne (1910–70) as a form of humanistic psychology. It aims to simplify and improve understanding of how people communicate and interact in order to help people to make better informed decisions. TA is an interactional concept grounded in the assumption that we take current decisions based on past beliefs – beliefs that were at one time appropriate to our survival needs but that may no longer be valid.

The basic assumptions in TA are that awareness is an important first step in the process of changing our ways of thinking, feeling and behaving, and that all of us are in charge of what we do. Others do not make us feel in a certain way; rather, we respond to situations largely according to our beliefs.

The main concepts within TA (Berne, 1973) are:

▮ three ego states – parent, adult, child;

▮ the need for 'strokes';

▮ parent drivers;

▮ games;

▮ life positions and life scripts – I'm ok, you're ok.

A coach-mentor using a TA approach would:

▮ Advocate and explain the basic concepts and terminology to raise awareness.

▌ Carry out a 'script' analysis to clarify their life role.

▌ Expose the 'game playing' and inappropriate 'drivers' to try to achieve the I'm ok, you're ok position.

▌ Reject the childhood decisions and beliefs.

Systems theory

Systems theory was first proposed by Ludwig von Bertalanffy (1901–72) who saw that systems are interrelated and interact with their environments, and through this interaction they evolve.

In systems theory it is necessary not only to understand the individual parts of a system, but also to understand the relationships between those individual parts. For example, it is not enough to consider how people think separately from their emotions – rather they must be considered together to understand the relationships between them.

An example that highlights how the systems theory works is the coaching process itself, as one session can very often create an immediate change in an individual. Whether this change is positive or negative, or whether it is apparent straight away or not, an individual who has changed will react to the environment in a different way, which then has an impact on the environment, as well as on the individuals who inhabit that environment.

Systems theory will become of increasing importance with the recent growth in team coaching. A team is a good example of a complex system. One possible implication of applying this theory is the suggestion that individuals should not be coached in isolation but always in the context of the team or group (system) in which they work.

HOW DO WE APPLY OUR UNDERSTANDING OF DIFFERENCES TO OUR PRACTICE?

Having accepted that everyone is different, thinks and behaves differently and needs to be approached differently, how can that understanding be used in practice?

Psychometric assessments

Psychometric assessments have been increasingly used as a means of building awareness about an individual's preferred approaches. Individual coaches may favour the use of particular psychometric tools, such as the MBTI, Firo-B, SDI and the Enneagram, to name just a few. Many coach-mentors also use various 360- or 180-degree feedback processes. All have the objective of enabling the coach-mentor and the learner to understand the individual better so that they may work together more effectively.

Advocates of psychometrics claim a number of benefits of using such tools, such as helping the individual to build self-awareness; highlighting motivations that may not be obvious; providing clarity about strengths; identifying the particular preferences for the way he or she perceives and makes judgements about the world. Once again in our view it is not necessary to be an expert in any single psychometric tool to become an effective coach-mentor. But it is important to have a general understanding of their potential use and to have access to a more qualified colleague if a situation appears likely to benefit from their expertise.

Modelling excellence (NLP)

If you wanted to become very good at achieving particular results, a simple and rather common sense suggestion might be to copy the thinking and behaviours of other people who seem already to be performing at a high standard to achieve those results. If you studied enough people performing at these high standards, it should be possible to establish patterns of thinking and speaking that these 'experts' use repeatedly to obtain their results. It would then be relatively simple to train people to copy these patterns and therefore achieve similarly high results.

Two Americans, Grinder and Bandler, developed these ideas in the 1970s into a theoretical framework they christened Neuro-Linguistic Programming (NLP). This has grown into a worldwide 'movement' and has a direct application to the coaching and mentoring community.

Bandler and Grinder (1990) believed that although 'experts' have developed many innovative and effective skills, the core of their effectiveness was primarily the attitudes, approaches and philosophies they had in common that made them capable of effective work.

As such, NLP has developed its own methodology and philosophical approach towards being effective within the human world, born out of pragmatism rather than theory.

One part of the explanation of why NLP has become a 'movement' is that these theories have been developed in many ways and new adherents are usually taught to believe and operate from a core set of 'presuppositions'. A typical set might be any combination of the following:

- It is possible to communicate with a person's unconscious and this is the most powerful communication.

- It is impossible *not* to communicate.

- The meaning of communication is the response you get.

- The words we use are *not* the event or the item they represent.

- The mind and the body are one system and affect each other.

- The map is not the territory. There is a huge difference between the world as it is and the world as we experience it. We create a representation of the world that suits us. If one changes one's internal map, one changes one's experience of the world.

- One should respect another person's model of the world.

- Language is a secondary representation of one's experience. When we communicate we give only 1 or 2 per cent of what we have actually experienced. The language we use is 'twice removed' from the world as it is.

- The best quality information is behavioural.

- All behaviour is oriented towards adaptation and has as its origin, a good intention.

- The law of requisite variety states that the element of the system that has most choice is the element that controls the system.

- You are in charge of your mind and therefore the results.

- Each person has all the resources they need.

- The perceived frame around a situation gives it its meaning.

▌ There is no failure only feedback.

▌ Human beings are more complex than the theories that describe them.

Many professional psychologists and other practitioners are very sceptical about NLP because of the lack of accepted scientific support. We understand those reservations but also acknowledge the positive views of people like Nick Blanford, a Learning and Development Manager in a City of London legal firm who summarized the debate well during an online discussion we recently participated in:

> I think that NLP does create quite polarized views. Before I embarked on my NLP studies I was very sceptical about it so decided to train as practitioner to find out more. I have witnessed some quite alarming uses of NLP, which I think is a real shame and I think some of the NLP evangelists do it a disservice.
>
> In short, however, I feel NLP is a set of tools and techniques which have the potential to be tremendously positive for the learner. For me coaching is far wider than staying at the non-directive end of the spectrum, although this is the space I prefer to occupy most of the time. I do bring elements of NLP into my coaching which includes some time-line work, hypnotherapy, certain questioning techniques and lots more.
>
> My challenge has been to blend these techniques into my traditional coaching which I feel I have achieved. Used properly NLP doesn't get the learner to dwell in a negative state as some psychotherapy has a tendency to do. NLP is much more about understanding ourselves better and then looking forward rather than backwards.
>
> I have used NLP to help people look at very difficult situations and reframe the experience into a more positive one by seeing it from the perspectives of others. Sometimes this new level of awareness is the only thing that has helped the learner move forward. I have found NLP to be an exceptionally useful part of my toolkit as a coach and I think it has made me much more effective both personally and professionally.
>
> But as has been said, it's horses for courses; some will love NLP and some with loathe it. Either way is fine as long as you have fully explored it and come to your own conclusions based on facts rather than hearsay.

General conclusion on awareness of individual differences

While we have not explicitly evaluated each approach in terms of effectiveness or efficacy, we have found it difficult to quantify how a specific coach-mentoring approach compares with other psychology or philosophy models.

These approaches all provide valuable insights and we believe the good coach-mentor needs to understand the underlying psychology or philosophy in order to draw from them appropriately in his or her coaching practice. However, over-reliance on one approach can produce a one-dimensional style of coaching. There is value in multiple styles and the demonstrated flexibility of the coach-mentor.

A coach-mentor needs to be able to hold multiple perspectives in mind and to look at challenges and issues from different viewpoints. Underpinning this concept is the view that there is no single truth about what enables a person to change, but rather a series of constructions that are more or less useful for evoking change.

This leads us to a common sense conclusion that successful coach-mentors will be guided more by the situation they face than by following any single theory or dogma. They will have the knowledge, skill and confidence to be able to adjust their style flexibly, even in the course of a single conversation, in response to the situation they are facing. To do this they will, of course, need to be able to understand, interpret, respect and sometimes apply techniques from all competing brands and approaches that contribute to the emerging coaching and mentoring profession. As Carl Jung (1998) said: 'Learn your theories as well as you can, but put them aside when you touch the miracle of the living soul. Not theories, but your own creative individuality alone must decide.'

6

Feedback that builds confidence and success

At its most basic, the success of coaching and mentoring depends largely on the quality of communication between the people involved. Workplace communication has long been recognized as an important topic, yet two decades ago it was treated largely as a matter of language and techniques. People were trained in presentation skills, letter or report writing and telephone techniques. Today this is recognized as inadequate. The topic, now often termed 'interpersonal communication', covers a wide area of understanding about how humans interact.

Effective communication still depends on the correct choice of words and methods. A logical structure with the right level of content, plus the manner, tone and pace of delivery are still important. However, it is now recognized that more breakdowns in communication occur because of psychological relationships than because of the 'mechanics' of communication.

Put simply, in any communication situation people bring a whole range of important 'filters' that can distort the reception, understanding, acceptance and response to messages. Figure 6.1 aims to simplify some of these complex interactions by highlighting some of the key 'filter factors' that messages have to pass through on their two-way flow between senders and receivers.

Figure 6.1 Filters

The diagram is only one-dimensional and perhaps suggests a systematic and linear flow through the process. In practice, interpersonal communication is not so smooth and many of the elements interact with each other in different ways, depending on the specific situation. For our purpose of becoming effective coach-mentors, the main lesson is not to underestimate the sensitivity and care that is necessary to achieve mutual understanding, acceptance and motivation to respond positively to messages we send and receive.

One definition of human communication is: 'the passing and receiving of messages between two or more people in order that both sender and receiver may act appropriately on their interpretation of the messages they receive'. The beauty of this definition is that it stresses that communication is a two-way process that leads to appropriate action. However, it also emphasizes the equal importance of responding to what is sent and that feedback is fundamental to effective communication.

In the context of coaching and mentoring to develop learners and their performance, it is not an exaggeration to describe feedback as 'the fuel that drives improved performance'. Feedback can drive motivation to continue and develop in two directions. Get it wrong and motivation goes backwards fast. Get it right and motivation goes steadily forward towards achieving the goal.

Feedback can be defined as communication with a person that gives information about how his or her behaviour is perceived by others and the effect it has on them. Feedback helps us to learn by increasing both the awareness of what we are doing and how we are doing it. Being able to seek and receive feedback about performance is therefore an important skill for learners too. If sought and accepted, it will greatly increase their self-awareness by helping to build a more accurate picture of how they are perceived, and it will help them to monitor the progress of their learning and development.

OBSERVING PERFORMANCE

Coach-mentors will continually find themselves having to give feedback. Inexperienced learners often want to ask, 'How well am I doing?' or, 'Have I improved my competence?' while an experienced learner, attempting to improve his or her performance still further, might say 'If I do it this way, I think it will be better. What do you think?' Alternatively, a coach-mentor may be asked, 'I have the chance to apply for this new job, do you think I should do it?' Deciding on the appropriate feedback in these situations needs careful thought and should be based on the following principles:

1. To encourage the learner to articulate his or her own answer to the question.

2. To establish just how important or relevant the coach-mentor's feedback will be.

3. Having encouraged self-assessment, to give feedback which is clear, concise and constructive.

Constructive feedback increases self-awareness, offers options as well as opinions and encourages self-development. It does not mean giving only positive feedback on what a learner has done well. Feedback about poor performance, given skilfully, can be equally useful and important as an aid to development. Feedback may well result in people:

▮ understanding more about how they come across to others;

▮ choosing to change;

▮ keeping their behaviour on target to achieve good results;

▮ becoming more effective.

POTENTIAL BARRIERS TO EFFECTIVE FEEDBACK

There are several barriers to both giving and receiving effective feedback:

▮ Feedback can come as a surprise or shock when there are no clear objectives for the job or development, or when the learner and the coach-mentor do not share the same perception of these.

▮ The feedback may be delivered in a way that the recipient sees as concentrating on critical or unsubstantiated judgements, which offend the recipient's sense of fairness.

▮ There may be a problem of credibility; it is important that the recipient believes the feedback-giver is competent to comment on those points.

▮ Previous history of receiving negative feedback may make the recipient feel obliged to 'defend his or her corner'.

▮ People are 'afraid' to give feedback because they are not confident about handling the response and are concerned that feedback will damage relationships.

Sensitivity and stress

Many young people are shy and feel awkward and embarrassed in new situations where they have to perform alongside other experienced staff. More experienced people on a learning programme can also feel inhibited and unable to relax in the same way that they can in their usual work role. Helping people whose self-image may not be too high by guiding them towards early successes, encouraging positive behaviour and rewarding the efforts being made, will usually contribute towards the development of a positive 'I can do it' attitude.

Coach-mentors need to be sensitive to the mental state of the people they are working with. Of course, they must also be sensitive to their own mental state because feedback is a two-way process. In stressful situations, people react differently and not always in the most appropriate manner. It would be a mistake to underestimate how stressful some may find the coaching and mentoring session itself!

Transactional analysis

Transactional analysis (TA) is one approach to understanding the basics of the differing mental states that people have in relationships. A transaction can be defined as a signal or stimulus from one person to another, and the signal or response sent back in reply. One signal and its reply is followed by another, so that feedback becomes a series of transactions.

TA suggests that there are three predominant mental states and that we respond in any one of these states, depending on our mood and the pressure of the situation. The sensitivity of the transaction lies in recognizing, selecting or managing our own behaviour, thus responding in the most appropriate state to match both the situation and the mental state of other people involved. People continuously swap and change between the three states, which can be summarized as: parent (beliefs), adult (thinking) and child (feeling). Briefly, a description of each of these ego states is:

▮ Parent state – consisting of our beliefs, values, attitudes, standards and morals. We calculate and judge in this state. We can also adopt either a critical or caring outlook to the other person.

▮ Adult state – consisting of our rational, unemotional and analytical outlook. In this state we are happy to consider reality, facts and figures. We readily engage in problem solving and discuss calmly the implications of our decisions.

▌ Child state – consisting of spontaneous, fun-loving and natural reactions to events. We are curious, creative and jokey in this state. On the other hand, we may behave emotionally, irrationally, being petulant and sulky, just like spoilt children who can't get their own way.

Understanding the basics of TA and the ego states can help us to be aware of our mental state before or during a situation. This helps us respond in a way that is most likely to avoid the clashes that occur when transactions between ego states become crossed rather than complementing or parallel.

In constructive feedback, the aim is to get both people operating in their adult ego state. They can then review facts, examine solutions and implications without crossed transactions creating too many obstacles of beliefs and prejudices or feelings and emotions.

How would it feel to you?

A useful way to begin to understand how to give appropriate feedback in content, style and tone is to consider how you feel when you ask for or receive feedback. Ask yourself, when receiving feedback from another person, do you:

▌ Listen actively to their description of your behaviour or performance?

▌ Carefully consider what is being said, trying to see the situation from their point of view?

▌ Weigh up the positives and negatives of changing or modifying your behaviour?

▌ Enter into a calm discussion about your views on their comments?

▌ Mutually agree upon subsequent action?

▌ Ask for any support or help you think will be necessary?

▌ Thank them for their feedback?

Be honest. In many situations there are probably as many 'No' answers as 'Yes' ones. By reversing the role, it is easy therefore to see some of the difficulties we face as recipients of feedback. We may:

▌ Be afraid of what others think of us.

▌ Wonder about the motives behind the feedback. Is it honest? Can they be trusted?

▌ Fear a loss of face or independence even if we do recognize the need for help.

▌ Lose confidence and feel inferior.

If coach-mentors are sensitive to these issues and constantly remind themselves of them by 'looking in the mirror', they will avoid the pitfalls of insensitive and inappropriate feedback.

It may be all too easy for coach-mentors to take the relationship aspect of their roles for granted, particularly if they have been working with their 'learner' for some time. In the work situation, issues of power and authority often underlie working relationships: learners usually understand only too well that they are in a dependent and somewhat subordinate role vis-à-vis their coach and mentor.

It is not always easy therefore to create a relaxed, informal and supporting relationship. This is particularly true if the culture of the organization is bureaucratic or aggressively hierarchical and results-oriented. Recognizing the reality of pressures from the organizational culture is important since it will help both parties to develop realistic expectations. It is also important to appreciate the effects that differences in age, gender, educational background, ethnicity and culture can have. This is not to say that these are necessarily or inevitably obstacles, but simply to point out that lack of awareness and sensitivity of such issues may make feedback sessions strained and unproductive.

FEEDBACK THAT BUILDS CONFIDENCE

During a development process, one of the best ways to build confidence is regularly to monitor progress. 'How am I doing?' is a reasonable question that the learner will want to ask. For development to occur, the learner often needs to be reassured that he or she is beginning to perform closer to the standard or goal agreed earlier. Regular reviews act as a vehicle to reinforce effective performance, highlight areas for improvement and recognize developing strengths and potential weaknesses. Obstacles or barriers to performance can also be discussed and joint actions planned to overcome them or, if necessary, the development programme can be modified.

Whenever a development review takes place, it should start by agreeing exactly what it is that the learner wishes to discuss in relation to achieving his or her goals. If a qualification is the goal, how is the learner progressing against the syllabus or development plan? What do results from tutors' reports indicate? If the acquisition of new knowledge or skills is the goal, how has the learner performed in post-learning tests or in applying the information gained? A consistent, well-organized and systematic approach by the coach-mentor is one of the surest ways to build confidence in his or her learner.

Retaining control over situations or events for the duration of the development plan is crucial for it to be successful, but some things are often outside the learner's control. For example, a learner may find it difficult to resolve any conflicts caused by short-term reassignment of his or her work priorities and completion of the development plan over the original timescale. His or her manager may be under considerable pressure to achieve short-term results and find it difficult to give immediate priority to what he or she (the manager) may see as the learner's medium-term development needs.

To maintain progress and help to encourage a positive attitude, it is necessary to help learners to develop strategies to marry their needs with the organization's pressures. Review sessions should also get the learners to highlight achievements and reflect on difficulties that have been overcome. Comparing progress to the original plan and recognizing the passing of milestones helps to show real step-by-step achievement. This also provides an excellent opportunity to reward and celebrate successes. This will, in turn, reinforce the growing confidence in the learner.

Aspects that the learner has had difficulty with should be discussed honestly. Was it the method or style of instruction or coaching that caused problems? Were the targets for achievement set too high? Was the learner trying enough or perhaps trying too hard? Were there sufficient chances to practise before starting the activity? By breaking down what may appear to the learner to be an insurmountable and complex problem into smaller chunks will allow each part to be simplified and dealt with separately and more successfully.

Observing performance

Successful coach-mentors should look at both the 'what' and the 'how': they should consider the results the learner achieves and the process he or she used to achieve the result. One of the most effective ways to do this is to actually watch the learner in action. This allows the coach-mentor to observe his or her performance directly, rather than depend on the second-hand information of others, who might have added their own interpretation to the behaviour. Sometimes the learners themselves have only a partial understanding, or even a misunderstanding, of how they perform or behave. Direct observation enables the coach-mentor to be precise in identifying specific behaviours, techniques or skills for further development.

Observing performance is best done on a regular, recurring basis to offer ongoing validity to your coaching feedback. A little feedback and guidance close to the activity is more effective than storing up the feedback for the once or twice a year formal performance review. However, learning how to observe your learners without making them feel intimidated or uncomfortable is a skill in itself. Here are some tips to consider when planning to observe behaviour.

Simplicity tips – how to observe

1. Start by explaining, or confirming if previously agreed, why you are observing the learner – you are there to help him or her improve, not to catch him or her out. Make sure you also explain your purpose to any other people directly involved.
2. Be aware of your influence on the learner's performance and position yourself as unobtrusively as possible. Consider how you would feel if someone was watching you do something.
3. Observe the process the learner is using to carry out the activity.
4. Observe the quality or standard of the final outcome or end result achieved.
5. Don't interrupt the interactions or activity, or distract the learner or any other participants during the observation.

---

6. Ask questions to verify your understanding, but only when you are sure you are not affecting the activity or process.
7. Observe the interaction or behaviour several times in different contexts if possible.
8. Make notes at the time for discussion later.
9. Compare what you saw with any 'standard' procedures or with what you may have previously been told.
10. Observe other people carry out the same process or behaviour for comparison purposes if relevant or appropriate.

OBSERVING A TEAM

In recent years there has been an increase in coaching complete teams rather than individuals in isolation. There is an argument that all coaching should ideally be done in the context of the 'team' since most business activities are now done as some form of teamwork. Trying to coach individuals while ignoring the context of their 'team' or 'teams' is likely to be limited in effectiveness. The power and influence of the rest of the team are such significant factors that they cannot be ignored. Therefore, most individuals should be coached as part of their team and ideally the whole team could be coached together.

When coaching and observing a team rather than an individual, there are several additional factors to take into consideration. As the coach-mentor, you will probably be observing the whole team in action, performing their function as a team. When observing and giving feedback to a team, it helps to consider this four-stage process:

1. Contract: What role do they (the team and the sponsor) want me to play? Am I clear on what I am looking for?

2. Observe: How do I behave when watching the team's behaviour?

3. Diagnose: Do I understand what I am seeing?

4. Intervene: Should I intervene now? How? Why?

Considering this process in more detail raises a number of important questions that coach-mentors should ask themselves at each stage.

Stage 1. Contracting

Who are the stakeholders?

The first thing to consider is that in a team situation the client may or may not be a member of the team. You may have been brought in by a senior manager to work with one of his or her teams. You may have been brought in by the leader of the team or a team member who is not the designated leader. Alternatively, you may be the leader or a member of the team who wishes to, or has been asked to, take on a coaching role for the benefit of the whole team. In all cases it is important that you are clear at the start what the current situation is and what is expected. So ask yourself: who is the client? Who are the stakeholders? What is their stake?

▌ The team leader? Is their leadership in question?

▌ All the members of the team? Is the team united? Do they all accept the need for coaching?

▌ The sponsor? If they are not part of the team, are they part of the problem?

▌ All or some of the above? In some cases, the coach-mentor may be working with a combination of the above.

▌ Are there any conflicts or contradictions? Do all parties want the same thing?

▌ Do you have a clear contract? Be clear that you understand what each stakeholder believes is the situation and what needs to be done.

What is my contract?

The next part of stage 1 is to consider what the team are willing and prepared to work on. There are five levels of interaction associated with any team that need to be considered before starting to work with the team members. The five levels opposite are of increasing sensitivity and require increasing levels of diplomacy and tact from the coach-mentor:

1. Structural-functional: focuses on the attitudes, values, beliefs and perceptions about the roles and functions of members with little regard for individuals' characteristics.

2. Performance-goal: focuses on the appropriateness and commitment to the performance goals of the team.

3. Process: focuses on processes and looks at the changing work behaviour and work relationships between members of the team.

4. Relationships: focuses on attitudes, feelings, values, beliefs, perceptions and behaviours of the individual members and the relationship they have to other members of the team.

5. Intrapersonal: focuses on self-awareness, the attitudes, values, beliefs and perceptions that each member has about themself. This level of intervention is usually best handled individually in one-to-one sessions separate from the team.

Stage 2. Observation

Once you are clear on what you are looking for and this has been agreed with all concerned, it is necessary to prepare for the actual observation and consider the following:

▌ Do I join the team or keep out of the way? Are you expected to take part in the discussion or activity of the team? If you are the team leader or a member of the team, not taking part might be difficult and disrupt the normal working of the team. On the other hand, can you objectively observe what is happening and focus on the interactions while also performing a team function? It may be advisable to agree with your team colleagues that you 'step out' of the activity in order to give more comprehensive feedback. It is easier for a coach-mentor who is not normally a member of the team to take a passive observer role.

▌ Am I keeping an open mind? When observing a team in action, it is important not to prejudge people, jump to conclusions, argue or interrupt. Teams have their own culture and dynamics and their own way of working.

▌ Am I aware of my own emotions? Try to listen and observe objectively even when you might disagree with what is being said or done. It is vital to suspend your own prejudice and not allow the fact that you disagree with what is happening to influence your observations.

Stage 3. Diagnosis

The purpose of your observation is to infer the correct meaning in what you are observing. Therefore, it is important to ask the following questions before considering a suitable intervention:

▌ Have I observed the behaviour for long enough to make a reliable diagnosis? Is this a persistent behaviour or a one-off? Be aware that feedback will not be accepted if the team can dismiss it as an aberration from their normal behaviour.

▌ Is my diagnosis within the boundary of my contract? Is what I have observed appropriate to the level of interaction I have agreed to provide feedback on? The team will resent feedback at an inappropriate level.

▌ Can I describe my observations without judgemental comment or tone? Can I say what I have noticed without implying what I observed was wrong or inappropriate? If the team believe they are being criticized, they may respond defensively.

▌ Am I articulating something the team members have recognized for themselves? Do the team seem to be aware of what is happening? If you describe something they have noticed for themselves your feedback is more likely to be accepted as valid.

Stage 4. Intervention/feedback

Having decided there is something worth feeding back, you need to consider the best time to give your observations. Ask yourself:

▌ If I do not intervene now, what is the probability that I can intervene later and still help the team avoid the negative consequences of continuing the dysfunctional behaviour?

▌ If I do not intervene now, will another team member intervene? If this happens, is it likely to make the situation better or worse?

▌ Is the observed behaviour central enough or important enough to warrant intervention?

▌ Have I already contracted with the team to make this type of intervention? Do I have their permission?

▌ Will it help or hinder their learning and/or the performance of the team?

▌ Should this intervention be handled individually or would it be best to speak to them privately?

▌ Do the team have sufficient experience and knowledge to use the intervention to improve their effectiveness, or would it just confuse and frustrate them?

▌ Are the team mature and open enough with each other to handle the intervention positively, or would the intervention cause more friction and dysfunction?

▌ Do the team have enough information (or can I give them enough information) to make an informed choice on how to respond to the intervention?

▌ Will the team have time, or are they too overloaded, to process the intervention?

HANDLING THE FEEDBACK SESSION

There are clearly a range of ideas and techniques that can be used to build confidence and the will to succeed, and the key is deciding when any of them might be appropriate. How feedback is handled on a day-to-day basis is therefore crucial.

It is important for the coach-mentor to always be aware of the necessity for giving negative messages with positive ones wherever possible. Strengths should be balanced with weaknesses and the aim should be to be fair as well as totally honest. It also helps to keep feedback as immediate as possible. The question of timing is crucial, particularly if the session is likely to be disappointing – don't delay it and don't give feedback in small amounts. You needn't mention every single fault, but you should concentrate mainly on the essentials. If you start with 'picky' less significant points, you may create an atmosphere that makes the discussion of more important topics unnecessarily difficult.

If, as we have previously discussed, you are asked for your advice, you should give it, but remember that some of us like to give advice because it makes us feel important. Sometimes this only serves to satisfy our ego. Similarly, you should avoid trying to persuade or even argue. If the other person becomes defensive or obstructive, try to discover the reason for this reaction and build on that towards a positive action.

Be aware, too, that over-praising is often dangerous as it can confuse the situation. Being supportive does not mean constant praising, but rather creating an atmosphere in which learners can admit faults or fears, knowing they will be understood if not necessarily endorsed.

Always strive to be sensitive to the other person and avoid un-wittingly denying the individual his or her feelings with hasty comments like, 'You don't mean that' or, 'You have no reason to feel that way'. It helps, too, if you can keep your comments as descriptive as possible and avoid making value judgements or giving the appearance of making a personal attack. Avoid saying, 'What a stupid way to do it'; try rather, 'On reflection can you think of a better way of doing it?'

Some tips are easier to give than to apply, but they will all produce a positive response. It is equally important to recognize that other behaviours have the potential to destroy the value of the feedback you give. For instance:

▌ being quick to disagree;

▌ being overly critical;

▌ being distant or aloof;

▌ interrupting repeatedly;

▌ ignoring comments, ideas, feelings;

▌ not asking any questions at all;

▌ appearing to be in a hurry to finish the session.

There are a number of things, too, that learners can do to ensure that they get quality feedback:

▌ Identify who is best placed to provide them with feedback – managers, coach, mentor, suppliers, customers, colleagues. The concept of 360-degree feedback encourages an all-round look.

▌ Agree an appropriate time and place when they will be able to have a constructive discussion.

▌ Be clear about the areas on which they need feedback.

▌ Try not to cover too many things in one discussion, but focus on the key issues only.

▌ Challenge the person giving feedback if they feel they are not being completely honest or specific enough for the information to be useful.

▌ Ask probing questions of the coach-mentor to identify what behaviour they should continue doing or stop doing.

Be aware that, although giving feedback is a difficult and unfamiliar process for some people, most will welcome the fact that you have sought their views and are willing to help.

Having sought feedback from their coach, mentor or another person, learners must ensure that they receive it skilfully and assertively by:

▌ listening actively, concentrating and being receptive; this will make it easier for the giver to be honest;

▌ clarifying and testing their understanding of what is being said;

▌ not reacting defensively or trying to justify their behaviour;

▌ spending some time reflecting on the feedback received;

▌ thanking the person for the feedback.

VISUALIZING SUCCESSFUL PERFORMANCE

An extremely powerful way of increasing motivation and enhancing the will to succeed is to teach learners how to visualize themselves performing an activity successfully and smoothly. Before attempting the task, encourage them to use their mind's eye and project themselves forward in time to see themselves doing the task in the way they would like to perform.

Sportsmen and women often use this technique and visualize themselves carrying out each action in slow motion. They concentrate on mentally rehearsing each step and then grooming it until it is perfect. Whenever the action is unclear or hazy, they re-run this mental video until a perfect sequence is logged in their memory bank. This allows them to relax when they actually perform and rely on their memory to steer them to a successful result.

In a business context, this technique can be adapted to help nervous presenters. Get them to visualize themselves:

- talking fluently to the audience;

- hearing their words putting a point across persuasively;

- seeing their gestures adding emphasis;

- watching their amusing anecdote draw smiles and appreciation from the audience.

This will help build up the confidence that they will be successful when they come to perform in 'real-time'.

HARNESSING THE ESSENTIAL MENTAL QUALITIES

Building confidence, then, is about harnessing the mind of the learner. In Gallwey's book *The Inner Game of Tennis* (1974) he talks about the two 'selfs' that are part of a performer's character. Self one is the 'teller' who instructs, evaluates and tries to control the performance. Self two is the 'doer' who actually performs the task, often unconsciously and automatically.

In Gallwey's sporting analogies, you can often see and hear the two selfs having a conversation. Self one is usually exhorting self two to try harder and to do specific things, as well as criticizing what is happening. This can get in the way of self two's natural flow and ability by creating a 'busy mind' and distracting the performance.

For the learners, the danger may be that they try too hard and so complicate and confuse themselves with too many of their own instructions. Poor results then encourage self-doubt to creep in, which can begin a downward spiral. The secret is for self one to trust its other half and simply let it perform. Self one demands a role, however, so the learner must programme it with images of the task and of performing it successfully. Holding back on criticism and replacing this only with observation allows self two to make subtle adjustments and perform better.

Whitmore, in his book *The Winning Mind* (1987), takes this process further. He has developed a list of what he describes as the 'essential mental qualities':

- Responsibility: taking personal responsibility for both successes and failures and not blaming other factors. Responsibility empowers the learner to take action, not wallow in recriminations.

- Awareness: most simply described as focusing on what is going on around you while performing. Being conscious of all factors in the environment and in the body allows learners to self-correct their actions.

- Concentration: involves remaining in a passive state while focused on the task, but staying receptive to ideas and thoughts. By not trying too hard, learners avoid the anxiety and pressure on themselves.

- Relaxation: aids containing self one by keeping the chatter and instructions to a minimum. When learners let concerns about the future or regrets about the past into their mind, they also let in anxiety.

- Detachment: involves learners standing apart mentally from the activity and observing their actions. Maintaining a free and flexible state keeps self one at bay.

- Commitment: encapsulates the will to win in three steps. First, the goal must be achievable to the learner. Second, obstacles to achievement must be eliminated. Finally, the will must be supported by 100 per cent honest effort.

- Trust: by being fully prepared, learners can trust their own mind and body to reproduce the action or task. Self two takes over the driving seat and lets self one merely observe how well the performer has done – without judgement.

These concepts, although relatively easy to explain, are really quite sophisticated to apply and require careful study and practice. However, they are important ideas to master and employ.

A final tip for the learner, which Whitmore advocates, is to find a personal stimulus that creates a positive and relaxed mind and to use it either as an outlet before or during the activity. Examples might include listening to a favourite piece of music on a personal stereo or recalling an inspirational poem. Physical activity, such as a visit to the gym or a short run, can have a relaxing effect too. All of these techniques, Whitmore believes, help people to understand and capture the essential qualities of the mind and support a confident and positive approach by the learner.

MAKING WINNERS

Giving feedback that helps to build confidence and success is not simple. Done effectively, feedback is about the making of winners. It fuels the motivation to learn how to improve performance – your main aim as a coach-mentor. Think carefully before you start to give feedback. Remember, it is fundamentally a two-way process. When in doubt, try to put yourself in the recipient's place or, to quote the proverb: 'Do unto others as you would be done by.'

The following checklist should help you to apply the essentials of giving effective feedback.

Essentials of effective feedback

1. Remember you get more out of people if you are sensitive to their situation and treat them as adults.
2. Imagine how you would feel if you were on the receiving end.
3. Make your feedback honest as well as fair.
4. Balance negative and positive messages.
5. Don't avoid weaknesses, but always balance them by emphasizing strengths as well.
6. Choose the appropriate time and place as well as the appropriate tone and language.
7. Keep criticism simple and constructive by concentrating on behaviours, not personal attitudes or beliefs.
8. Encourage people to take responsibility for their own development.
9. Be well organized yourself and hold regular progress reviews.
10. Recognize that you may be taken as a role model, so practise what you preach.

7

Observant listening

There is an old saying that God gave us two eyes and two ears but only one mouth so that we could look and listen four times as much as we speak. Certainly, we have increasingly realized that talking is not the main part of the communication process. Not everyone appreciates this, however. How often have you attended communication courses where the tutor spends most of the time explaining how you can structure your presentation or use visual aids but little, if any, on improving your listening skills?

More attention is also often paid to developing your observing rather than listening skills. If you have ever participated in games or exercises where several people are shown the same picture and asked to describe what they see, you will know that it often results in contradictory interpretations. All kinds of obstacles impair visual communication – and not just poor eyesight! People's expectations, assumptions, prejudices, values and wishes, all influence the messages they receive from observing and listening. Coach-mentors rely heavily on these skills and therefore need to be able to apply them effectively.

A coach-mentor using a 'hands-on' style needs, for instance, to listen to a learner's reply not only for accuracy, but also for the note of confidence or hesitation in the learner's voice. It is this that will confirm whether he or she has really understood the coach-mentor's message.

Confidence and other emotions are most likely to be expressed as much in the tone of the response as in the actual words themselves.

A coach-mentor using a 'hands-off' style relies very heavily on questioning skills. As soon as the question is asked, the coach-mentor has to listen to and interpret the response and at the same time decide very quickly on the next appropriate question. Pausing to reflect on the answer is often a sensible technique, but having to ask for the answer to be repeated because of lazy listening will damage the coach-mentor's credibility and effectiveness.

Coach-mentors will sometimes hold sessions in their own office. Failure to take the elementary precaution of arranging for phone calls to be diverted can result in unnecessary interruptions to listening, as well as signalling a certain lack of interest in the purpose of the session. A coach-mentor focusing on developing a specific skill often has to observe and judge actual performance in the workplace against a clear framework of competence standards and then immediately follow the observation with questions to check understanding. If awarding a qualification for the skill is involved, and is to have credibility and validity, it is essential that any number of coach-mentors observing the same demonstration of performance and listening to the same answers would make the same judgement as to the competence of the performer. So the consistent application of these skills to a high standard is a requirement for effective coaching and mentoring.

IT ISN'T SIMPLE TO OBSERVE

The first rule of observation must be: 'It isn't as simple as you might think.' Observing is not necessarily a step-by-step easy-to-follow process, but is often continuous with lots of things happening at once. Take the example of the coach-mentor during a session with a horse rider preparing for a competition. Just imagine what that coach-mentor would have to observe while the rider was practising even a simple movement:

▮ What aids did the rider use?

▮ How did the horse respond?

▮ What went well and why?

▮ What went wrong and why?

▮ How could it have been improved?

▮ Was the pace right?

▮ Was the rider's position right?

▮ Did the horse keep a correct outline?

▮ Did the horse resist and why?

▮ What was the general overall impression?

Take another example of a coach-mentor observing a salesperson in a sales interview:

▮ How did he or she greet the customer?

▮ What was the initial reaction?

▮ What type of questions were asked?

▮ How well did the salesperson listen?

▮ Which products were presented and in which order?

▮ To what extent was the customer involved?

▮ How were the sales aids used?

▮ Did the salesperson handle technical questions knowledgeably?

▮ How did the salesperson gain commitment or take an order?

▮ What was missing?

▮ How did the customer react throughout the interview?

▮ Which aspects of the interview went well?

▮ What could have been done better?

These and many other observations have to be noted as they occur. Learning to concentrate and interpret what you see is really hard work. Working with a checklist prepared in advance helps enormously. Note-taking is also essential: relying on memory means that important points are sometimes missed.

Taking notes is not easy for some people but, with practice, the skill can be acquired. Noting key words or phrases is one technique, while using mind maps is another. Having a sensible-sized pad and a pen available is an obvious tip that is sometimes forgotten.

These two examples of a coaching situation also illustrate another difficulty associated with observing. Had the coach-mentor become actively involved with either of the instances described, it may have reduced the validity of the observations and subsequent feedback or assessment. Unobtrusive observation and restraining the impulse to intervene and take control when things are not going exactly as you think they should, are therefore also important skills to develop if you really want to help people to learn from their own experiences.

Another danger to be aware of is failing to distinguish between an observation of behaviour and making an inference, or drawing a conclusion, about the cause of the behaviour. The examples in Table 7.1 illustrate the potential pitfalls.

Table 7.1 Observation vs inference

Observation	Inference	Real cause
John attended the meeting in shirt sleeves	He is unprofessional	He got soaked in a rainstorm
Wendy always leaves work right on time	She is uncommitted	She has a difficult childminder
Ken entered the figures in the wrong column	He is careless	The forms are poorly designed
Anne disagreed strongly	She is bad-tempered	She is under severe stress at work and at home

These simple examples show how easy it would be for a coach-mentor to misread the situation. The guiding principles are that observations must be objective – make an accurate record of non-judgemental, actual behaviour – and that inferences are subjective; avoid drawing conclusions and stick to descriptions of what you see.

THE IMPORTANCE OF OBSERVING BODY LANGUAGE

Imagine a situation where you, as a coach-mentor, choose to hold a session with two people at the same time. This could be at the end of a project or before a programme starts. One of them sits with his or her arms folded, feet tapping and replies in a terse but perfectly accurate way. The other person is sitting forward comfortably, arms on the table, looking you straight in the eyes and answering calmly but in an equally accurate way.

If you are listening only to the verbal answers, you will receive one set of messages and quite possibly only gain a partial view of the whole picture. However, by observing consciously at the same time, you will also receive what are described as 'non-verbal' messages. These messages can be equally important and may give clues to either unspoken frustrations or important development needs.

To help resolve these dilemmas, it is important to appreciate the basics of non-verbal communication, or 'body language'. Facial expressions, gestures, posture, eye signals, body movements, all transmit a message. A useful book that gives more information on observing body language is *The Definitive Book of Body Language* (Pease and Pease, 2004). Body language, it is claimed, can be a window to our thoughts; indeed it often speaks louder than words – we may say one thing, while our bodies say another.

Some of the key non-verbal signs are as follows:

▌ Empathy can be signalled by smiles, open and positive gestures, standing or sitting close, eye contact or nodding and tilting the head.

▌ A defensive or distrusting attitude can be signalled if someone sits with his or her crossed leg towards you, while a willingness to trust can be signalled if the crossed leg is away from you.

▌ Anger or aggression can be signalled by a rigid or tense body posture, staring eyes, clenched fists or clasped hands, tightly folded arms, foot tapping and finger pointing.

▌ Nervousness can be signalled by downcast eyes, hand over the mouth or frequently touching the face, shifting weight or fidgeting.

▌ Boredom can be signalled by picking imaginary fluff from sleeves, pulling at an ear, stifled yawning or gazing around the room.

One word of caution however: you will note that we have said only that these signals can indicate the different emotions. One gesture on its own almost certainly won't be enough to give the full picture. Rather, it is a combination of non-verbal signals that you need to learn to interpret. When the combination of non-verbal signals appears to suggest a specific emotion that matches the words this is known as 'congruence'. Where there appears to be a mismatch between the non-verbal signals and the language used by the learner, this is described as 'incongruent' and, as such, is a possible cause for concern. Of course, not only must we recognize all these gestures in others, but we must equally be aware of our own body language as it may be interpreted by others in the same way!

It is also important to remember that, although people in the same culture or from the same country send and receive similar non-verbal signals, people from other cultures or countries may interpret them differently. For example, in the UK, people signal numbers with their fingers by using the index finger as number one. However, in Germany, if you put up your index finger for a beer in a bar, you're likely to be served two – they use the thumb to signify number one. Another example of cultural differences is that an ok signal formed by creating an 'O' with your finger and thumb means ok to the English or Americans, but to the French it means zero or no good at all! As an example of cultural differences, the eye contact rules used by Africans for showing interest and paying attention are opposite to those of Europeans, who often misinterpret this different behaviour as rudeness or sullenness. Styles of spoken communication can also differ markedly. Certain Asian groups tend to give very detailed responses, which are sometimes considered by non-Asians to be irritatingly long-winded.

One also has to be careful about other people's speaking delivery, which may be affected by simple awkwardness rather than any attempt to mislead. If someone has an irritating or squeaky voice or speaks slowly or in what you find to be a boring manner, it will be even more important to listen to the message rather then be distracted by the delivery. It is the message that has to be judged, not the way it is said, and this can sometimes be an incredibly difficult discipline to achieve. 'It ain't what you say but the way that you say it' can be dangerous advice to the listener!

AWARENESS OF PERSONAL SPACE

There is another aspect of body language that should be considered within our context. This is the need to be sensitive to the area or space that people claim as their own, as if it were an extension of their body. People tend to regard their office, desk, chair and the space surrounding any of their possessions as 'their territory'. To make yourself at home by immediately sitting down and placing your belongings on their desk may well be offensive and invasive to that person.

Therefore, coach-mentoring learners in their office or 'territory' may make it difficult to take them out of their comfort zone, when appropriate, as they may feel too mentally comfortable. Conversely, a coach-mentor should consider the effect on both themself and the learner of running the session in the coach-mentor's own office or 'territory' as the learner may feel intimidated or mentally unsafe.

There are also what are termed 'personal zones' or 'interpersonal space': an invisible ring or sphere in which we live as individuals, within which we don't want others to encroach or come too close. These are often determined by culture or personality and therefore the size of this space will differ between individuals. As a rule, this space is jealously guarded by us all. Move within the interpersonal space of somebody and he or she may well immediately feel uncomfortable and even threatened – unless of course you share an intimate personal relationship! Research has shown that people from the country need greater interpersonal space than people from towns and cities. Another example is entering a crowded lift. You will notice that often, if it is very crowded, people tend to look up at the floor level indicator light, or down at the floor, rather than at each other, mainly because they feel too close together. Research suggests that these behaviours relate to the very strong reactions that such invasion of body space can cause. If you want people to feel at ease in your presence, keep to the distance within which people feel most comfortable. An arm's length is a good guide.

It is also important to think carefully about the positioning of desks, tables and seating arrangements for a mentoring or coaching session. A competitive or defensive position may be created when a desk or table forms a barrier between two people sitting directly opposite each other. They are forced quite literally to take sides. This does nothing to enhance openness, trust and harmony. To avoid this, salespeople are often encouraged to move round to the customer's side of the desk when demonstrating or illustrating a particular point. This is done to create a feeling of togetherness as opposed to a 'you-and-us' relationship. It also allows customers to avoid the salesperson's face so that, if necessary, they can look away with ease. This sales technique has to be handled with care to avoid the negative reaction of invading personal space, but it is a useful technique for coach-mentors to be aware of.

TRUST AND DISTRUST

Eyes often give the most accurate and revealing signals of all. The expression 'we see eye to eye' indicates that agreement can be signalled by eye contact. Acceptable eye contact is usually in the area of 60–70 per cent during the course of a conversation. If the other person either hardly looks at you or alternatively stares intently at you all the time, there is a tendency to immediately regard him or her with distrust and suspicion.

It is claimed that body language can be the most important part of any message. Some estimate that it accounts for at least 55 per cent or even more. When the words spoken conflict with the body language, it is claimed that the receiver tends to believe the non-verbal message. For example: you are busy but a colleague asks you for a few minutes of your time. You easily agree: 'No problem, I've always got time for you.' Soon, however, you are looking at your watch and shifting in your seat. All the signals suggest you haven't got the time, despite what you have said. If your colleague is alert and sensitive to these gestures, he or she will curtail the conversation and leave rather than risk upsetting your relationship. Similarly, how many times have you seen a child look at the floor and deny that he or she has 'done wrong'? You may be strongly inclined to believe the stance and gestures, not the verbal denial.

MYTHS AND PREJUDICES

It is also important to guard against your own prejudices and to avoid stereotyping people when interpreting visual and verbal messages. Some people, for instance, believe that people with public school accents or who wear glasses are automatically cleverer than other people. Another common myth or fallacy is that older people find it harder than young people to learn new things, or that women managers make emotional decisions while male managers act only on logical and rational interpretations of factual information.

When you stop to think about these issues, it soon becomes clear that they are highly unlikely to be true, but there is a real danger of allowing stereotypes, or simply first impressions, to affect your judgement. In a situation where you are assessing performance against a standard, this can be particularly dangerous as you need to listen and observe throughout the session to make an objective judgement.

Of course people can try to mislead you. Someone who answers in a confident manner or appears to agree with everything you say may create a more positive impression on you than his or her level of performance deserves. There is a well-used term called the 'halo effect' that describes this possibility. This warns of the danger of allowing one impression or element of the skill being demonstrated to create an overall impression that 'clouds' all the other evidence. It is suggested that we are all open to this type of misjudgement, particularly where one strong negative impression blinds us to an accurate and objective interpretation.

ACTIVE LISTENING

We have concentrated so far on observation skills, but many of these issues also relate to listening. So let's discuss listening in more detail. It is useful to recognize that there are different levels of listening:

- *Peripheral* listening is done at a subconscious level and can occur in formal or informal situations. For example, you may be in a busy restaurant talking to people at your table, but also picking up snippets of conversation from another table.

- *Apparent* listening is what we all do most of the time. We look as if we are listening, but in fact we are not really concentrating.

- *Active* or effective listening is often what we should be doing. This involves really concentrating on the message being transmitted by trying to understand not only what is being said but how and why it is being said.

It is the ability to listen 'actively' that separates the good communicators from the poor. Like any skill, effective listening requires self-discipline and practice and it is certainly hard work. It is estimated that most people talk at a rate of 125 words per minute, but that they can think at up to four times that speed. This means that as a listener you have spare mental capacity which, if you do not discipline yourself, results in your mind wandering and a lack of concentration.

We have probably all experienced ourselves tuning in and out of conversations or discussions and then having to ask for something to be repeated because we have missed a key point of the message. A listener can, however, use his or her speed of thought to advantage. You can learn to use the time to summarize mentally what the speaker has said, to ensure you have understood the message fully and to consider whether you need to ask any further questions.

Success as a coach-mentor depends to a large extent on the ability to concentrate efficiently on what is being said, often for long periods. You may well make the other person feel unimportant or insignificant if he or she senses that his or her ideas and feelings are not being paid close attention to. The relationship will then undoubtedly suffer. The temptation to only half listen is, of course, very real. Having asked a question, if you get an early indication that the answer is going to be correct, or is exactly what you were expecting, there is an inclination to switch off before the end of the response. By doing so, you risk missing some enlightening new information or ignoring additional information that shows that your initial assumptions were incorrect. Similarly, you may be so preoccupied formulating your next question that you miss at least part of the response to your current question. Therefore, to be able to actively and deeply listen you must ensure your own mind is quiet, with your whole attention focused on the person speaking. You should be fully present but not trying to anticipate what is being said or influence the direction of the conversation. This state for a coach-mentor is sometimes described as 'simply being and not doing'.

So what does active listening involve? What do we mean by active listening? This deep level goes beyond simply listening to what the other person said, into the area of intuition, insight and almost telepathy. Understanding this process will help you to adopt a disciplined approach to active listening. The process is as follows:

1. Having received a response there is interpretation of what was heard.

2. This leads to understanding.

3. Then comes evaluation, or weighing the information, comparing it with existing knowledge and deciding what to do with it.

4. Based on your understanding and evaluation, you react by planning your reply.

5. Finally, you respond.

What cannot be ignored in this process is, of course, the way in which a response is delivered. It is estimated that tone counts for as much as one-third of a message. Active listeners must be alert to any emphasis on certain words, also to fluency, or lack of fluency, as well as any emotional language. In the same way, they must listen for the meaning behind the words. If a learner says, 'The main reason is...' this could imply there are other considerations that may need exploring. Only by active listening will it be possible to identify and evaluate what is not being said.

Active listening requires planning and practice. We have to work at it and, like all other skills, we need to be interested and motivated enough to want real results from our efforts. So, how do you go about putting all this into practice? Let us suggest a three-stage process for efficient listening.

Stage 1. Carefully select the location (whenever possible)

▌ Choose a quiet room or area free from the distraction of other people and noise.

▌ Arrange seating to avoid any physical barriers, such as a desk, but don't sit too close.

▌ Set aside any other work you are doing.

▌ Arrange for telephone calls or messages to be diverted.

▌ Remove or ignore any other distractions.

▌ Shut the door, if possible.

Stage 2. Create the right atmosphere

▌ Make sure the speaker knows you want to listen to him or her, look interested and maintain eye contact without staring.

▌ Give the speaker your full attention.

▌ Address the person by the name he or she wants to be called, usually his or her first name.

▌ Be patient – allow the person time to say all he or she wants to say (within reason).

▌ Maintain a relaxed posture and encourage the speaker to feel relaxed.

▌ Be encouraging by leaning forward, nodding, putting your head to one side, smiling whenever appropriate.

▌ Empathize as necessary if something difficult or painful or different from your own beliefs is being discussed.

▌ Don't take any views personally and try not to be defensive.

Stage 3. Practise helpful listening behaviour

▌ Make listening noises: eg 'Mmmm', 'Yes', 'I see'.

▌ Pause before responding to indicate that you are digesting what has been said.

▌ Keep an open mind – do not prejudge people, jump to conclusions, argue or interrupt: other people may have a different point of view.

▌ Be aware of your own emotions; listen carefully even where you might disagree.

▌ Suspend prejudice; don't allow the fact you disagree make you turn a deaf ear to what is being said.

▌ Concentrate on what matters by trying to get at the core of the response.

▌ Be sensitive to mood, facial expressions and body movements to understand the full meaning of what is being said.

▌ Plan to make a report to someone else following the meeting and imagine he or she is the sort of person who likes to know all the details of what you have heard.

▌ Seek more information by summarizing, asking questions, repeating or paraphrasing.

▌ Summarize to check your understanding.

Finally, make a habit of taking notes. As we have seen, listening only occupies something like one-quarter of our available mental capacity. The remaining three-quarters of the mind will wander if not otherwise used. More importantly, note-taking gives you a record of what you are hearing and helps to emphasize the importance you are placing on what is being said to you. Many of the helpful behaviours we have listed will be made easier by good and accurate note-taking, but it helps if you explain to the other person why you are taking notes.

TELEPHONE COACHING

Increasingly, coaching and mentoring is being done over the telephone because of the pressures of time and the additional cost of travelling to a common meeting place. Also, remote working is becoming more common in organizations, which means that many people are using the telephone as the 'normal' form of communication with colleagues, customers and suppliers. Telephone coaching has the benefit of not being location-dependent and so can be done across different countries or even continents. This form of coaching offers increased flexibility for both learner and coach-mentor but would appear to make active listening much more difficult. Many coach-mentors say they could not possibly do telephone sessions as the vital component of being able to see, and react to, the learner is missing.

We would challenge this assumption. Until the widespread use of video telephones or web-cam technology, it was true that you could not actually see the learner during a session. However, you can still fulfil nearly all the requirements of active listening over the telephone. By ensuring the session meets the requirements of the three-stage process described earlier, the coach-mentor and learner can experience a totally satisfactory session. Let us consider those same three stages.

Stage 1. Location

▌ All the requirements apply, apart from don't sit too close!

▌ An addition requirement is a hands-free telephone, or headset. It is not advisable to hold a conventional telephone to your ear for an hour or more!

Stages 2 and 3. Atmosphere and behaviour

▌ Again all the requirements apply with the exception of maintaining eye contact without staring.

▌ We would say that you will need to increase the verbal cues as a reinforcement for the non-verbal signals. Comments such as, 'Yes, I am still listening', 'Go on', 'I'm still here,' will encourage the speaker to continue to talk and to reassure him or her that you are still on the line.

▌ You may think some of the requirements are not important or irrelevant in this section since the other person cannot see what you are doing. However, it is amazing how much of a person's body language can be detected by actively and deeply listening over the telephone. We believe that continuing the body posture and non-verbal mannerisms you would normally adopt when actually facing the person should be maintained. In this way your concentration will be increased and something of these supporting behaviours will be detected by the learner. Some coach-mentors find placing a picture of the learner, or a suitable object in front of them to focus on aids this process. Others find closing their eyes to minimize the distractions of the coach-mentor's own surroundings helps their concentration.

We believe that coach-mentors need to feel comfortable with, and competent in, using the telephone as an integral part of their practice. Telephone coaching should not be seen as a poor substitute for the real thing to simply save time or money. It should be seen as an equally valid alternative to face-to-face sessions and offered as an integral part of the relationship with the learner. For example, some learners said they preferred telephone sessions because they felt able to be more open and reveal more of themselves without the embarrassment of being 'looked at' by the listener.

Having said that telephone sessions are just as effective as face-to-face sessions, we do strongly recommend that the first session with a new learner should be face-to-face if at all possible. We would also recommend the last session should be face-to-face if possible and practical.

Whether you are a coach or mentor, effective observing and listening is key to both roles. If you listen actively, your learner will feel listened to. The coach-mentor will want to encourage responses that guide learners to work out the best way forward for them. The following checklist should prove a useful guide to improving the way you use your eyes and ears.

Simplicity tips – effective observing and listening

1. Non-verbal signals are important and you should learn to recognize them to get the full picture.
2. Beware of cultural differences in communication habits.
3. Recognize that your own emotions affect the signals you send.
4. Don't let your own values, attitudes and beliefs get in the way.
5. Concentrate and pay attention to details.
6. Take accurate notes to avoid misunderstanding.
7. Tone of voice is often as important as what is said.
8. If you want to understand you must be prepared to listen and show you are listening actively.
9. Establish the performance criteria before you begin to observe or listen to the performance.
10. Plan in advance to avoid distractions.

8

Questioning

One of the oldest jokes we can remember is the story of the little boy standing outside the door of a house. A door-to-door salesman approaches him and asks, 'Son, is your mother at home?' 'Yes,' replies the little boy. The salesman knocks on the door but receives no reply. After several minutes of knocking with no response he turns angrily to the boy and says, 'Hey, I thought you said your mother was at home.' 'She is,' replies the boy, 'but I don't live here!'

The moral of that story is that if you don't ask the right question, you probably won't get the right answer. The combination of asking the right question because you know the subject matter well, and asking the right question in the most appropriate way, lies at the heart of skilled coaching and mentoring.

Coach-mentors should bear in mind that their primary role is to help and encourage their learners to develop. This cannot be achieved if they create undue pressure or confusion by inept questioning. A meaningful coaching or mentoring session depends on using questions that provoke a response that enhances learning. It is important to build a relationship that is open and honest, so that the learner can accept the sometimes painful process of being stretched by difficult questions. Asking embarrassing questions is likely to lead to defensive, negative responses and a deterioration of the relationship.

Developing good questioning skills is vital to successful coaching and mentoring. Many managers will, during the course of their work, have received training on asking questions on interviewing, appraising and counselling courses. There are also plenty of written materials and learning packages available. Let us nevertheless look at various questioning techniques, which every coach-mentor should know about and try to apply.

UNDERSTANDING THE BASIC TYPES OF QUESTION

The importance of recognizing that there are two main types of question – open and closed – is a significant basic theoretical concept of questioning.

A closed question is one that may be answered by a simple 'yes' or 'no' and usually begins with 'do you', 'are you', 'have you', and so on. It may also be a question to which the respondent is offered a choice of alternative replies, such as 'Which of the following three alternatives would you choose…?' Open questions are aimed at provoking an extended 'free' response and might start with 'what', 'where', 'which', 'why', 'how' or 'when'.

Closed questions are appropriate:

- where a straightforward 'yes' or 'no' is enough;
- to gather or verify information;
- to confirm understanding of facts;
- to confirm agreement or commitment;
- to get a decision when there are only two alternatives.

The repeated use of closed questions needs to be avoided, however. A series of such questions can become very wearing on the respondent and can quickly turn a discussion or session into an interrogation.

A more difficult skill to develop, but one that is essential to guiding and supporting a learner, is to use open questions. These enable the questioner to:

▌ establish rapport and put the other person at ease;

▌ free up respondents to answer as they choose and in their own words;

▌ encourage uninhibited feedback;

▌ help to explore opinions and values in more detail;

▌ create involvement and commitment;

▌ check out the learner's understanding more comprehensively.

For example, if you wanted to ask someone his or her opinion on, say, the merits of the local football team, you wouldn't say 'Do you agree that the local team is a good one?' This invites a simple 'yes' or 'no' response. On the other hand, if you had phrased the question 'What do you think are the good points about the local team?', you would instead invite a response that required the candidate to express an opinion. If there were no good points, you then have the opportunity to follow up with 'Well, can you describe their weak points?' The benefits of using appropriate open questions are that you obtain more information and encourage the candidate to think more – a win–win result.

A VARIETY OF USEFUL QUESTION TYPES

Coach-mentors need to exercise care in selecting the best type of question to use in different situations. First they need to ask themselves some basic questions about the purpose of their questioning:

▌ Are they helping learners to explore their situation in more detail?

▌ Are they encouraging them to move from an overall analysis of their performance to a more detailed one?

▌ Are they looking to help learners to identify strengths and weaknesses that could be capitalized upon or improved for better performance?

▌ Are they working to increase personal awareness and responsibility?

There are several different types of questioning that are appropriate for different purposes, discussed below.

Awareness-raising questions

If coach-mentors want to encourage learners to develop their performance, they also have to help them to develop self-awareness, a sense of responsibility for future action and a commitment to persevere with the action. You will find that open questions like, 'What happened?' and, 'Why did that happen?' tend to produce descriptive and potentially somewhat defensive responses. On the other hand, questions like, 'How did it feel when you were doing that?' or, 'What do you imagine it would look like if you did it differently?' or, 'What can you do to lift the performance still further?' will encourage responses that focus on positive ideas for future action. We would call these 'awareness-raising' questions.

Reflective questions

This type of question is a useful means of eliciting clarification and confirming that you are listening 'actively'. By 'replaying' the words used by the learner or rephrasing and reflecting them back you, as coach-mentor, can both test your own understanding and encourage the other person to talk more. You can say, 'You said xyz…, can you explain in more detail please exactly what you mean there?' or you can use questions like, 'So is what you're saying…?' or, 'Let me just check that I understand you correctly…'. These types of questions give the opportunity for the respondent to give additional information or to think of new ways of making his or her views clearer. It also assures him or her that you have heard and understood correctly.

Justifying questions

These questions provide an opportunity for further explanation of reasons, attitudes or feelings. Examples are, 'Can you elaborate on what makes you think that…?', or, 'How would you explain that to someone else…?' This type of question can provide very useful responses, but can also appear rather confrontational, especially if delivered in a challenging tone or manner. Sometimes it is better to phrase them slightly differently, such as, 'You say this,… am I right in understanding that what you mean is…?' or, 'Could you help me to understand your explanation by putting it another way?'

Hypothetical questions

These are questions that pose a situation or a suggestion: 'What if…?', 'How about…?' These can be useful if you want to introduce a new idea or concept, challenge a response without causing offence or defensiveness, or check that you fully understand the implications of an earlier answer. Hypothetical questions can be very powerful and stretching in coaching and mentoring situations. However, they should only be asked when it is reasonable to expect the other person to have sufficient knowledge or understanding of the situation you are asking him or her to speculate about.

Probing questions

Effective questioning usually begins broadly and then becomes more focused on detail. Probing questions are those supplementary questions where the full information required has not been given as part of the initial response. The reason it has not been offered may be because the initial question was inappropriate, unclear or simply too general. Alternatively, the respondent may deliberately not be replying fully. Probing questions can also be used to discover motivations and feelings, where they have not been offered.

Probing questions are among the most difficult to ask and may, of course, involve asking a mix of open, closed, reflective, justifying and hypothetical questions. Their advantage is not only that they elicit more information where necessary, but they also help the learner to consider issues or factors that might be a little 'below surface'.

Two basic probing techniques are *funnelling* – where you start with large, broad questions and gradually narrow the focus down to the specific information you are seeking; and *drilling* – where you decide in advance the question areas you want to pursue and dig deeper and deeper until you strike the response you have been looking for.

Checking questions

Sometimes it is necessary to check what you are hearing or to correct an understanding. This can be done through a number of different open or closed questions, such as, 'Are you sure about that?' or 'This may generally be the case, but I wonder if it is true in your situation?' Or, 'Why do you interpret it that way?'

It is crucial, however, that the coach-mentor does not dictate the route of the discussion by 'forcing' its direction or be seen to be 'testing' through inappropriate questioning. Questions should be used to help learners to work on their own goals and needs and to take responsibility for them. Questioning should not be used simply to satisfy the curiosity of the coach-mentor. Questioning is about helping learners to explore possibilities and reach their own decisions; it should also be used to encourage self-development.

It is obvious, therefore, that coach-mentors should always use simple, uncomplicated and understandable language and also to make sure they do not make unfair or unrealistic assumptions or jump to conclusions.

TYPES OF QUESTIONS TO BE AVOIDED

There are several types of questions that are inappropriate for a coach-mentor to employ. These will not help to generate trust and they may provoke a negative, defensive or ambiguous response. Avoid asking:

▌ long-winded questions – they will probably be misunderstood;

▌ several questions rolled into one multiple question – people inevitably choose the easiest answers first and avoid the difficult one you really wanted to know the answer to;

▌ leading or loaded questions – they usually only demonstrate what you already know or think rather than what the respondent really understands or believes;

▌ trick questions unless you can explain the purpose – they can cause resentment and demotivation.

QUESTIONING TECHNIQUES

It is very difficult to give examples of the type of questions that might be appropriate for specific coach-mentoring sessions, since each session will be different and will need the coach-mentor to apply his or her general theoretical understanding and range of skills to meet the requirements of that specific situation. However, there are some techniques that may be helpful in the most common situations that a coach-mentor can face, such as:

▋ coaching an inexperienced learner to develop a new skill;

▋ finding time to help someone to sort out a problem when you as the coach are under pressure from a heavy workload;

▋ coaching an experienced and able learner who has the time and motivation to improve his or her performance;

▋ coaching a learner who is uncertain or unwilling to face up to awkward or unpalatable options;

▋ coaching someone who has little confidence or self-belief;

▋ coaching someone who is struggling with his or her work–life balance.

For each of these situations different questioning techniques can be employed. We'll look at each of them in turn.

Coaching inexperienced learners

One technique that has been found most helpful in these situations is called the 'Practice spiral' (once again, please remember that this is a model, not a set of instructions to be used in any and every situation).

The practice spiral starts with an initial explanation and demonstration stage. This is followed by a stage for reflecting on the learning achieved during the initial stage. Then comes a reviewing stage that focuses on drawing specific conclusions about how much progress has been made towards achieving the eventual goal. The final stage involves planning to practise again. This, of course, leads to another new experience, but this time at a slightly higher level of performance. The whole process begins again and continues to spiral towards higher and higher levels of performance after each new practice session. The process is shown in Figure 8.1.

There are a number of key points for the coach-mentor to follow at each stage of the spiral.

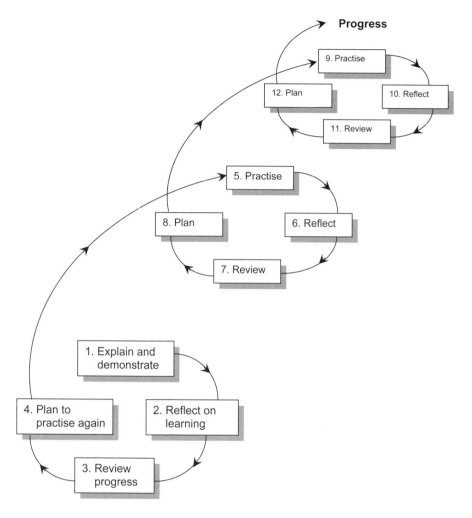

Figure 8.1 A practice spiral

Stage 1. Explain and demonstrate

At this stage the coach-mentor should:

▌ Summarize what is about to be explained and demonstrated.

▌ Emphasize why it is important.

▌ Outline how it is going to be done.

▌ Explain and demonstrate, following a logical sequence.

- Summarize, re-emphasizing why it is important.

- Allow time for questions, clarifications and feedback to check understanding.

Stage 2. Reflect on the learning

This stage should be deliberately timed. Often, simply allowing a few minutes private thought, note-taking or handling of a piece of new equipment is all that is required.

Stage 3. Review progress

At this stage, the coach-mentor needs to remind learners of the ultimate goal of the learning programme and to encourage them to articulate the progress they feel they have made so far. Skilful questioning can help learners to identify any barriers to learning they are experiencing, as well as enabling them to clarify any areas of misunderstanding that may have arisen.

Stage 4. Plan to practise again

Opportunities to practise what has been learnt are crucial to ensure that the required competence standards are achieved. The coach-mentor should ensure that there are three types of practice sessions:

1. *Risk-free opportunities:* where mistakes can easily be made and remedial action taken with no damage done or blame expressed.

2. *Close-observation opportunities:* where learners can practise in real life situations with the coach-mentor in close attendance to be able to intervene to help to correct any faults and to build confidence with constructive feedback and praise.

3. *Spot-check opportunities:* where the learner is free to operate in a real life situation but with the knowledge that there will be occasional spot-checks by the coach-mentor to offer feedback and motivation.

As learners progress up the spiral, the type of practice session the coach-mentor will agree with the learner will obviously move from risk-free to spot-check. Note that although the spiral starts with a totally hands-on style, the coach-mentor moves steadily down the styles continuum towards a hands-off position.

The 'skills framework' technique

The 'Spiral' technique works well when the inexperienced learner has to acquire a mechanical skill or has to master a new operating process. But when a 'soft skill', like presentation or influencing, has to be learnt or when a combination of process and soft skills, like interviewing skills and techniques, is required, it is more helpful to use a 'framework' technique.

This requires the coach-mentor to have a clear competency framework of the identified learning need on which to focus the development programme. As an example, let us choose the need to develop 'Appraisal interviewing skills and techniques'. This could develop the competency framework as in Figure 8.2.

This framework is a general checklist, which would be backed up by a more detailed set of checklists, and provides both the learner and the coach-mentor with an opportunity for a rigorous self-assessment of exactly what the outcome of the learning programme should be. Those areas that the learner already understands and in which he or she can perform confidently can be ticked off, allowing the coach-mentor to focus on those issues that need detailed attention. The coach-mentor now follows the normal coaching process model to achieve the required results.

This technique has the benefit of clearly showing that different aspects of the skills and techniques of the development programme will require different learning opportunities to be taken. Some will involve individual study, others observation and practice. While it may be an advantage for the coach-mentor to be a skilled interviewer, it is not absolutely necessary. The framework provides the coach-mentor with a clear overall appreciation of the desired outcomes and, if necessary, the learner can be given access to alternative and more detailed expertise.

One coach who has used the 'framework' technique to develop customer service telephone effectiveness (combining soft and process skills) is Elizabeth Harris, Managing Director of Groom House Training and Development. She comments:

Appraisal Interviewing Skills Framework

Please tick appropriate column

	Yes	Needs Help

Process knowledge

The learner understands:

		Yes	Needs Help
1.1	The purpose, benefits and limitations of appraisals		
1.2	The organization's appraisal process:		
	▪ Principles		
	▪ Practices		
	▪ Paperwork		

Process skills and techniques

The learner can:

		Yes	Needs Help
2.1	Collate and evaluate performance measures (before the appraisal)		
2.2	Prepare for the appraisal (in the weeks before)		
2.3	Brief the team members to prepare themselves		
2.4	Prepare for the appraisal (on the day)		
2.5	Follow a clear structure for the interview		
2.6	Provide feedback on performance during the interview		
2.7	Set objectives during the interview		
2.8	End an appraisal appropriately		
2.9	Help team members who have performance problems		
2.10	Provide ongoing support to achieve results		

Personal skills, style and attitudes

The learner can:

		Yes	Needs Help
3.1	Communicate effectively during the appraisal		
3.2	Resolve conflicts during appraisals		
3.3	Display a positive attitude towards personal development throughout the appraisal process		

Figure 8.2 Appraisal interview skills framework

I am involved in three different development situations. I coach my staff to manage their own learning and performance improvements; I coach-mentor a client to achieve a qualification and I also coach others to develop specific customer service skills.

Each situation calls for a different approach, and I find that a competency framework approach produces the best results when I am helping to improve performance in a specific skill area. It combines a rigorous analysis of the behaviour and performances that are required with an easy-to-use observation and self-assessment checklist. It also helps to ensure consistency of performance, providing all the coaches have a common understanding of the framework before they start coaching.

Remember, that in call centre situations, we may be talking 100 coaches, each aiming for the same quality of performance and so consistency is important. To achieve this, there needs to be not just a common understanding of the competences, but for fairness as well. There is therefore a need for regular meetings in which the group of coaches run check assessments to test for fairness and consistency.

One approach we use is to listen to recordings of customer interactions and then independently complete the checklist. Each decides the coaching priorities and discusses them with the rest of the group. If we are doing the job properly, we should all be agreeing on the priority areas for both improvement and reinforcement. We also run role-plays of the coaching meeting to ensure that feedback is given in a constructive way.

Elizabeth is a firm believer that coaching can be seen as the 'glue that makes training stick', particularly when the objective of the intervention is to improve something like customer service effectiveness over the telephone. As she points out:

In these situations the customer service representatives usually need a combination of product knowledge, technical dexterity to operate a computer program and personal skills. Knowledge can often best be imparted in a training context, but technical and personal skills require continual practice in real-life situations. Thus a combination of training and coaching will produce the best results. Organizations that try to save short-term costs by limiting the development to a training course alone usually find that it is an expensive mistake.

We then sometimes find ourselves in a situation where coaching to improve performance is seen as a 'punishment'. The truth is more likely to be either:

▌ Lack of the basic knowledge of how to do it.
▌ Misunderstanding the competences or objectives.
▌ Seeing no reward for doing the job.
▌ Factors outside the control of the individual.
▌ Being unaware of a performance problem.

As coaches, we have to be very careful to identify the root cause of the performance difficulty and work very hard to create the motivation to change behaviour. If the initial development programme had combined training with adequate coaching follow-up, these sorts of difficulties could have been avoided.

Coaching when you are short of time – the '3-D' technique

Even when an organization has followed the appropriate learning methodologies to develop its people, operational challenges still arise. For example, sometimes people ask for help at inconvenient times for the coach-mentor. Most managers are under increasing time pressures and may genuinely find it difficult to reorganize their priorities to meet the immediate needs of a member of their team. Experience has shown that coach-mentors who can cope with these situations are highly regarded by their colleagues and team members. Successful coach-mentors often express the belief that time spent in coaching to help with immediate problems is repaid many times over through the improvements in performance and higher levels of motivation.

The essence of handling these pressurized coaching sessions is to focus as rapidly as possible on potential solutions that the other person can recognize and take personal responsibility for implementing. The '3-D' technique is one that has been found helpful for these situations. It is based on recognizing a three-dimensional analysis, as illustrated in Figure 8.3.

To use this technique, a coach-mentor simply needs a blank sheet of paper or a flipchart. The learner is asked to quickly define the problem in a single sentence. Careful questioning and using the 3-D analysis technique enable the coach-mentor and the learner to quickly identify three elements of the problem under each of three headings:

1. the situation – eg timescales, lack of resources, geography;

2. people involved – eg unhappy customer, impatient boss, unreliable supplier;

3. you – eg lack of technical knowledge, conflicting priorities, the learner's general attitude.

With these three dimensions or aspects of the problem identified, it is usually relatively easy to identify several options to choose from, even

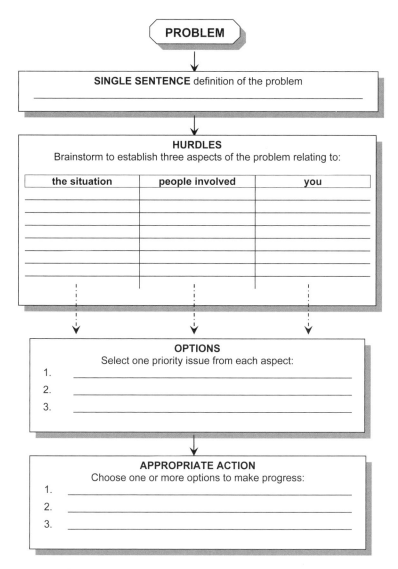

Figure 8.3 The 3-D technique

if most of them require actions related solely to the learner themself!
The final stage is to choose the 'best-fit' option to actually implement.

Following this structured technique, it is possible to focus rapidly
on potential actions. By relying almost entirely on questioning, the
coach can help people to articulate most of the issues and options
themselves. The coach-mentor will have enabled the learners to focus
more clearly and leave the responsibility for taking final decisions

with them. With practice, this technique can work in 10–15 minutes.

It is also possible to use the 3-D technique to coach yourself through a problem. You can try it for yourself now:

1. Define a current problem in a single sentence.

2. List three general issues relating to the problem situation.

3. List three issues relating to the people involved.

4. List three issues that relate specifically to you and the problem.

5. Choose one issue from each of your three lists of three issues.

6. Now identify one or more options that are most likely to make progress in solving the problem.

It may seem quite simple, but it works. The technique works best when the coach-mentor relies entirely on questioning to encourage the learner to work through the process.

Coaching an experienced and motivated learner – the 'GROW' technique

The GROW technique has its origins in sports coaches who have been influenced by Tim Gallwey's book *The Inner Game of Tennis* (1974). The technique relies heavily on using skilful questions and following a clear structure.

The idea of the GROW framework is to use a simple set of questions to guide the discussion through four stages of a coaching session or event. By going through the different stages, asking a variety of questions at each, you will be getting the individual to think about the issue/problem at hand and identify a possible solution, or range of solutions.

First, the questions focus on the 'Goal' the learners want to achieve in the immediate coaching session. Next, the focus is on the total 'Reality' in which the learners are operating. This is followed by questioning the practical 'Options' that the learners might choose, to achieve the goal that they have set themselves. Finally, the focus is on the 'Will' to actually take specific action to implement one or more of the options previously chosen. An easy way to remember the structure is to use the mnemonic that summarizes the GROW technique as:

> establish the **G**oal;
> examine the **R**eality;
> consider all **O**ptions;
> confirm the **W**ill to act.

Note: it might be necessary to retrace your steps through the stages if you realize the conversation suggests you did not fully explore a previous stage.

This type of approach is far more effective than simply telling learners what to do because it gets them to think about what they need to do and why they need to do it. The end result is that they feel more ownership of the solution, and therefore more accountable for taking it forward and making it work.

GROW is a powerful technique when you are coach-mentoring learners who already have a basic knowledge, expertise and enthusiasm for the issue involved. This is generally true in a sports context, but is often not the case in work situations. With inexperienced learners – or coach-mentors for that matter – the GROW technique is, in our experience, often too time-consuming and sophisticated for practical day-to-day work-based coaching situations.

However, where the coach-mentor has the time, patience and skills, the GROW technique is an excellent coaching technique for the 'hands-off' coaching style, with a proven record of success. The key is asking effective questions and systematically following the GROW structure during the coaching session. It is often an interactive process and cannot easily be rushed. The end result of coaching with GROW can be a highly focused and motivated learner.

Here is a selection of the types of questions that could be asked of such a learner, adapted slightly from the work of both Whitmore (1997) and Downey (2003).

Goal

To help establish the 'goal' that the learner wishes to focus on during the session, the following questions might be appropriate:

▌ What is the issue on which you would like to work today?

▌ What would you like to achieve by the end of this coaching session?

▌ How far and how detailed would you like to get in this session?

▌ Is your longer-term goal related to this issue?

▌ Is your goal SMART?

▌ Can we achieve what you want today in the time available?

▌ Are you sure you have defined your goal for this session?

Reality

To help the learner to understand more clearly the 'reality' of his or her own position and the context in which he or she is operating, the following questions might be appropriate:

▌ What is happening at the moment?

▌ How sure are you that this is an accurate representation of the situation?

▌ What and how great is your concern about it?

▌ Who, other than yourself, is affected by this issue?

▌ Who knows about your desire to do something about it?

▌ How much control do you personally have over the outcome?

▌ Who else has some control over it and how much?

▌ What action steps have you taken on it so far?

▌ What stopped you from doing more?

▌ What obstacles will need to be overcome on the way?

▌ What, if any, internal obstacles or personal resistance do you have to taking action?

▌ What resources do you already have – skill, time, enthusiasm, money, support, etc?

▌ What other resources will you need? Where will you get them from?

▌ If I could grant you one wish related to the issue, what would it be?

▌ Do you need to redefine your immediate or your longer-term goal? (If the answer is 'yes', you will need to start the process again.)

Options

To help the learner to fully explore a range of possible courses of action that are open to him or her, the following questions may be appropriate:

- What are the different ways in which you could approach this issue?

- What are the alternatives, large or small, open to you?

- What else could you do?

- What would you do if you had more time, a large budget or if you were the boss?

- What would you do if you could start again with a clean sheet, with a new team?

- Would you like to add a suggestion from me?

- What are the advantages and disadvantages of each of these in turn?

- Which would give the best result?

- Which of these solutions appeals to you most, or feels best to you?

- Which would give you the most satisfaction?

- Do you need to redefine your immediate or your longer-term goal? (If the answer is 'yes', you will need to start the process again.)

Will

To help a learner to reach a decision on the course of action that best meets his or her situation and to establish the learner's genuine commitment to follow through with action, the following questions may be appropriate:

- Which option or options will you choose?

- What are your criteria and measurements for success?

- When precisely are you going to start and finish each action step?

▌ What could arise to hinder you in taking these steps or meeting the goal?

▌ What personal resistance do you have, if any, to taking these steps?

▌ What will you do to overcome these resistances?

▌ Who needs to know what your plans are?

▌ What support do you need and from whom?

▌ What will you do to obtain that support and when?

▌ What commitment on a 1–10 scale do you have to taking these agreed actions?

▌ What is it that prevents this from being a 10?

▌ What could you do or alter to raise your commitment closer to 10?

▌ Is there anything else you want to talk about now or are we finished?

▌ When would you like to meet again?

We should stress that these are examples only, not a checklist of the exact number, type and sequence of questions that must be followed! Don't worry if you use different words – the idea is to empower the individual to take responsibility for his or her own actions. Remember – there is logic to the sequence of the stages: do not be ruled by the process, move back and forwards as the conversation develops but ensure the session ends up at 'Will'.

Uncertain or unwilling to choose – 'Transfer' technique

It is not uncommon for a coach-mentor to be faced with a situation during a session when it becomes clear that the learner is consciously and/or deliberately choosing to avoid answering questions that will make him or her face an awkward or unpalatable course of action. The action may involve the learner upsetting a close friend or colleague, disciplining a member of the team, or accepting that his or her personal ambitions are unrealistic or that his or her job is never going to be satisfying for them. In these types of situations the coach-mentor may believe that the learner's future positive development will only be possible if the uncomfortable truth is openly acknowledged.

The transfer technique involves transferring the responsibility for asking the awkward or unpalatable questions to the learner by using a phrase like: 'Can you help me by putting yourself in my position? If you were facing the situation where a learner was responding as you are, how would you handle the situation? What questions would you try to get the learner to answer or what suggestions or options would you encourage the learner to consider?'

We have found that, almost without exception, learners 'transfer' their behaviour, often in quite an assertive manner, and recommend a course of questioning or suggested options that force the issues to be confronted in a positive way. In the process of 'transferring' their behaviour, they often very quickly recognize the reality of their previous reactions and find it easier to resume the session in a new and more positive frame of mind. There is also a tendency to justify this behaviour change by using phrases like, 'Of course, the reason that I didn't decide that in the first place is…'. At that point, it becomes easier to probe further into their real reluctance.

The transfer technique enables the coach-mentor to help learners to free themselves from some of the inbuilt assumptions that are limiting their freedom to think differently. In this sense, the technique gets close to what Kline calls the 'incisive question' in her book *Time to Think* (1999). She writes: 'Over the years I have collected Incisive Questions that made a difference to people's lives and organizations.' Below are some samples. Note that the first part of the question asserts a positive assumption; the second part directs the thinker's attention back to his or her issue or goal:

▌ If you were to become the Chief Executive, what problems would you solve first and how would you go about it?

▌ If you knew you were vital to this organization's success, how would you approach your work?

▌ If things could be exactly right for you in this situation, how would they have to change?

▌ If you were not to hold back in your life, what would you be doing?

▌ If a doctor told you that your life depended on changing the way you lived, what would you do first for yourself?

These examples give just a glimpse of the powerful impact the skilful coach-mentor can have in liberating their learners' minds to think in completely new and potentially beneficial ways of the options that really exist for them.

Lack of confidence or self-belief: the 'Appreciative inquiry' technique

Appreciative inquiry was originally a theory for organizational development, developed in late 1980s and early 1990s by Cooperrider *et al* (2008). In recent years, with the growth of positive psychology, its potential as a coaching technique has become recognized, particularly where learners tend to see only the negative aspects of themselves or their situation.

When working with disadvantaged communities, Cooperrider and his colleagues noticed that the traditional problem-focused 'tell me what is wrong' approaches seemed to produce problem-centred answers. Therefore, they began to frame their questions differently: 'Tell me what is right.' They found this approach produced more positive and empowered responses, with the community starting to take responsibility for their own development. In this way the appreciative inquiry technique represents a viable complement to conventional problem-oriented approaches. The different approaches are illustrated in Table 8.1.

Table 8.1   Problem-solving process

Traditional Process	Appreciative Inquiry
• Define the problem	• Search for solutions that already exist
• Fix what's broken	• Amplify what is working
• Focus on decay	• Focus on the positives
What problem are you having?	*What is working well around here?*

The concept of appreciative inquiry is based on a set of assumptions described by Hammond in *The Thin Book of Appreciative Inquiry* (1998):

1.   In every society, organization or group, something works.

2.   What we focus on becomes our reality.

3. Reality is created in the moment, and there are multiple realities.

4. The language we use creates our reality.

5. The act of asking questions of an organization, group or individual influences them in some way.

6. People have more confidence to journey to the unknown future when they carry forward parts of their known past.

7. If we carry forward parts of the past, they should be what are best about the past.

8. It is important to value differences.

From the perspective of a coach-mentor working with someone lacking confidence or self-belief, these assumptions can be liberating:

▐ People's view of their reality will be shaped by what they persistently talk about.

▐ By inquiring about the best of the learner's past you can create a more desirable future.

▐ By asking about positive options and possibilities a coach-mentor can build confidence.

▐ A powerful positive image of ourselves will inspire us to action.

From these assumptions an appreciative inquiry technique of sequencing questions has been developed, consisting of four steps in a logical sequence similar to GROW. These four steps are:

1. Discovery.

2. Dream.

3. Design.

4. Deliver.

The following example illustrates how these steps could be applied to a coach-mentoring session.

1. Discovery: appreciating the best of what is

The purpose of this first step is to encourage learners to recall the conditions that surrounded and supported similar positive experiences in the past. This way you help 'anchor' their vision of a future situation to what has worked for them before:

▌ Recall positive experiences similar to your current challenge. What kinds of conditions were present during these positive experiences?

▌ Think back to a recent success. What did you do to make it successful?

▌ What was it about the environment/the community/the organization/the people that contributed to this good experience? What was your own contribution?

▌ Tell me about those times when you felt most productive, engaged, energized: how did that make you feel?

▌ What do you value about yourself as a professional and what you have to offer?

▌ What is the core factor that gives meaning to your work?

2. Dream: create in your own head the results of what might be

The purpose of the second step is to help learners imagine what their perfect future situation would look like. Having a clear vision of a desirable future will help them focus their development efforts, expand their potential and challenge any barriers:

▌ Imagine your current situation with everything going as you would wish it to be.

▌ What would the situation look like if all the factors were in place?

▌ What would your situation look like if all the factors that are most conducive to your performance were in place for you?

▌ What would the ideal outcome be for your dilemma?

▌ If your wishes came true, what would your perfect day be like?

▐ Imagine that some time has passed. What would your situation look like if everything had gone as planned?

3. Design: co-constructing the ideal

The purpose of the design stage is to help learners take their dream seriously for a moment and to produce imaginative ideas about what would need to happen for them to realize their dream. Thinking about innovative ideas will also help them define the dream in more detail. The coach-mentor should encourage them to be as imaginative and innovative as possible without worrying about being practical:

▐ Building on your previous positive experiences, how could you realize your dream?

▐ What ideas could be effective in helping you achieve your positive goal?

▐ What ideas could have high impact in shifting your current situation toward your ideal?

▐ Think of three things that would significantly change your situation and contribute to achieving your ideal situation.

▐ If you had a magic wand, what three changes would you make to improve the enjoyment and pleasure from your work?

▐ What are the main actions or elements contained in each of the previous ideas?

4. Deliver: realizing the dream by transforming your ideas into practical actions

The purpose of the fourth stage is to help learners decide what actions they will take immediately as practical steps towards their ideal goal, building on their ideas from the design phase. This is an iterative process where learners may need to revisit their earlier reflections. The actions should be realistic and as concrete as possible and only agreed if the learner is really committed:

▐ What actions are you ready to take to move towards your ideal?

▐ What will you seek to do?

▌ How are you going to make this happen?

▌ When will you make this happen?

▌ Who do you need to contact?

▌ Who else needs to be involved?

Imagining a positive future outcome built on past positive experiences is an important technique for countering initial negative images, beliefs and expectations.

Work–life balance: the 'Balance wheel' technique

As the name suggests, the balance wheel technique is particularly useful where learners want to work on improving the balance of parts or the whole of their life. The technique can be used in a wide variety of contexts; for example the wheel of life can be used where they wish to rebalance their whole life; the wheel of work can be used to improve the balance between different aspects of their work.

The technique consists of drawing a large circle and dividing it into eight wedge-shaped segments of equal size. Each of the segments of the wheel represents an important factor to the learner. An example of the wheel of life is illustrated in Figure 8.4 and the wheel of work in Figure 8.5.

Using the wheels

The example headings in Figures 8.4 and 8.5 are common to nearly everyone in the context of life or work. One or two segments should be left blank for the individual to put in what is important to him or her. The choice of headings for each of these factors should be up to the learner. This has two benefits: labelling some of the segments saves time in creating the tool and helps him or her understand what would be appropriate descriptors for the other headings. Alternatively, the learner could be shown a completed wheel as an example and then given one with no prescribed headings. This would acknowledge the importance of the learner feeling ownership of the headings by being able to choose what is important to him or her. However, this approach will be more time-consuming.

Each segment of the wheel has a scale of 0 – 10, with 0 at the centre representing total dissatisfaction and 10 at the outside representing

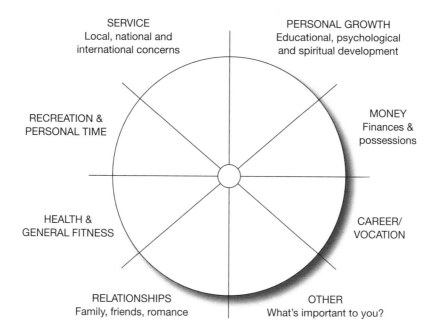

Figure 8.4　Wheel of life

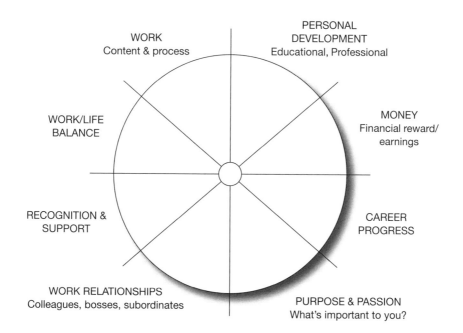

Figure 8.5　Wheel of work

total satisfaction with that factor. The learner is invited to shade in each segment to the degree to which he or she is satisfied with that factor of his or her life or work. Note that the important factor is the degree of satisfaction, not the amount of time spent on each factor or topic. The individual may not spend much time or energy on a certain section; he or she may be totally satisfied with that area and would shade it all in. Conversely, he or she may spend all his or her time in one area but be very dissatisfied; in this case he or she would only shade in a small part of the segment.

When the learner has completed the wheel, the relative size of the shaded segments is important to the diagnosis, and represents a new perimeter made up of the heights of all the shaded segments. The coach-mentor may want to ask such questions as: 'If the new perimeter of the circle represents your wheel of life, how smooth would the ride be, if this were a real wheel?' The implication is that significant variations in the size of each segment suggest a corresponding imbalance in their life and work. The joint exploration of what the completed wheel means for the learner should prove beneficial in helping him or her understand his or her situation and how to improve it.

The effectiveness of the technique lies in its powerful visual impact combined with the simplicity of its creation. Its use is easily explained to learners, who choose their own words to describe the segments of their wheel.

Simplicity tips – improve your questioning skills

1. Work hard to build rapport and put the other person at ease by adopting a friendly, supportive, helpful manner.
2. Be prepared to explain clearly why you need to ask questions.
3. Think about some questions in advance. However, do not be constrained by prepared questions. You need to be flexible enough to probe where necessary.
4. Try to ask clear, concise and specific questions but remember that open questions usually provide the most useful information.
5. Always acknowledge answers positively and in an encouraging tone.
6. Give answers real consideration before responding yourself. A pause will show that you have done so.
7. Use silence when appropriate (it may intimidate, so be careful, but it can provide additional, sensitive information as respondents may feel the need to keep talking).
8. Probe, where you need to, for extra information. Use phrases such as, 'Is that all?' or, 'Are you sure we have covered everything?'
9. Realize the importance of developing self-awareness by using questions such as, 'How did you feel as you did it?', 'When and where did you think your performance began to improve?' or, 'Why do you think you got that response?'
10. Always check your understanding by summarizing and using reflective questions.

9

An industry or a maturing profession?

We began this book by describing what we believe are the key influencers in the field of coaching and mentoring. In the previous chapters we hope we have made clear that applications and experiences of coaching and mentoring will be different in different international and cultural environments and that we cannot hope to do them all justice in this book. However, we believe there will be a 'convergence' of these key influencers over the next few years and that we will all benefit from learning from each other.

As such, we have called this chapter 'a maturing profession' since this increasing cooperation and collaboration across the profession is a clear sign of maturity. However, throughout this book we have used the term 'profession' and it is the use of this term that raises the fundamental question we will attempt to answer in this chapter, namely: 'Is coaching and mentoring an industry or a profession, or a sub-set of other professions?'

In attempting to answer this question, this chapter will examine the recent growth of professional bodies associated with coaching and mentoring, look at their motivation and mission, and try to predict their future. Before we do this, we will identify what we believe are the key requirements for a profession based on the models of other related professions, thus enabling us to map the current and predicted activities of the professional bodies against these key requirements and help provide an answer to the above question.

WHAT MAKES A PROFESSION?

Looking at professions in related fields, they appear to share several common features:

1. Body of academic and research literature.
2. Agreed statements of ethics, values and discipline.
3. Membership bodies with differing grades or levels and status.
4. Qualification requirements.
5. Continuing professional development requirements and criteria.

By considering each of these in more detail, it is possible to review what is currently happening in the world of coaching and mentoring and anticipate what might happen in the near future.

1. Body of literature

One of the features of a profession is a significant quantity of published academic and research literature; a profession must carry out and publish regular and rigorous research. A recent search on Amazon.com identified nearly 2,500 books on coaching and mentoring. Many of the coaching publications are by practising coaches sharing tips, techniques and their best practices in how to coach. Some of the evaluative research is produced by universities in various countries, but most is published by coaching organizations that wish to prove that their coaching has been beneficial to the organization. Understandably, there are some concerns about the independence and objectiveness of these studies when they are done by an organization that has a vested interest in showing coaching to have been successful. On the other hand, most coaching and mentoring takes place within commercial organizations and this can generate a reluctance by many to publish details of what goes on within their organizations.

However, we have recently noticed a growing number of journals containing academic research, independent evaluations and practical case studies of coaching and mentoring. Here are just a few:

Coaching: An international Journal of Theory, Research and Practice

Journal of Evidence Based Coaching and Mentoring

International Journal of Coaching in Organizations

International Journal of Mentoring and Coaching

Research Papers and the Coaching at Work Journal

The Coaching Psychologist

International Coaching Psychology Review

It would appear then that there is a significant and growing body of published literature across all aspects of the field. This is growing in quality as well as quantity, although research literature is still low. Interestingly, mentoring has considerably more research published than coaching. This is due to a number of factors:

- Formal mentoring programmes have been in place for a number of years.

- They are usually company sponsored and have administrative resources allocated, which makes the capturing and dissemination of the data easier.

- They are often set up with specific and common goals to be achieved and the achievement of these goals is closely monitored.

- Coaching programmes in contrast tend to be more individual and/ or low key, making large-scale research more difficult.

2. *Agreed statements of ethics, values and discipline*

All professions produce a statement of ethics and values that all members of that profession agree to abide by in their practice. These statements or codes are published by the professional bodies and adhering to the relevant code is a condition of membership. But is there an agreed code of ethics and values for coaches?

At the time of writing the answer would have to be that there is not a single code that everyone supports. However, there are a number of codes of ethics produced by coaching bodies such as the European Mentoring and Coaching Council (EMCC), the Association for Coaching (AC), the Association of Professional Executive Coaches and Supervisors (APECS) and the International Coaching Federation (ICF). Although these codes are not identical they do contain many similar statements, such as this one from the EMCC:

> The coach/mentor will acknowledge the dignity of all humanity. They will conduct themselves in a way which respects diversity and promotes equal opportunities. It is the primary responsibility of the coach/mentor to provide the best possible service to the client and to act in such a way as to cause no harm to any client or sponsor. The coach/mentor is committed to functioning from a position of dignity, autonomy and personal responsibility.

The codes also define and describe themes such as:

- *Competence* – training, continuing professional development and experience.
- *Context* – the relationships, expectations and contracting.
- *Boundary management* – referrals and conflicts of interest.
- *Integrity* – confidentiality, disclosures and the law.
- *Professionalism* – protecting the client, openness and exploitation.
- *Breaches of the code* – the complaints procedure.

So although there is not yet a single code of ethics and values, there are sufficient alternatives to enable any aspiring professional coach or mentor to find a code that matches his or her own values and philosophy.

3. Membership bodies, grades, levels and status

To be defined as a profession requires there to be one or more professional bodies to which members belong. These bodies should ideally set differing grades, levels and requirements for membership, monitor and maintain quality of practice, and provide forums for sharing good practices.

In recent years, a considerable number of professional bodies associated with coaching and mentoring have become prominent in the UK. Although in many ways very similar these tend to fall into one of three categories.

Category A

This covers a much wider remit and contains special interest groups. For example:

▐ British Association for Counselling and Psychotherapy (BACP) – has a Coaching Forum.

▐ British Psychological Society (BPS) – has a Special Group in Coaching Psychology and a breakaway group that has recently formed a Society of Coaching Psychologists.

▐ Charted Institute of Personnel and Development (CIPD) – has a Faculty for Coaching at Work as well as including coaching and mentoring in its standard professional qualifications.

Category B

This category contains other professional bodies that exclusively support coaching and mentoring in various contexts, such as:

▐ Association for Coaching (AC) – a powerful, marketing-led organization focusing mainly on the promotion of the services and development of individual coaches and the status of the AC as a professional body.

▐ European Mentoring and Coaching Council (EMCC) – individual, training, academic institutions and corporate members focus mainly on the quality and standards of coaching and mentoring across Europe.

▐ Association of Professional Executive Coaches and Supervisors (APECS) – a breakaway group from the EMCC that emphasizes the primacy of a psychotherapeutic approach to senior executive coaching, including a strict supervision regime for professional coaches.

- The International Coach Federation in the UK (ICF) – originally a United States-based organization focusing on the promotion and credibility of individual coaches, but now with a large international membership structure.

- The World Association of Business Coaches (WABC) – a Canadian and United States-based organization that promotes a distinctive business focus for coaching in comparison to a more holistic approach, such as that of the ICF.

All these professional bodies have different roles and purposes and therefore appeal to different groups of coaches and mentors.

Category C

In the UK, the government plays a significant role through the Quality and Curriculum Authority (QCA), which sets the standards for all academic and vocational qualifications. Academic institutions offer a range of qualifications but, in the vocational arena, the various Awarding Bodies apply National Occupational Standards (NOSs) frameworks.

NOSs describe what people need to do, know and understand in their job to carry out their role in a consistent and competent way. They are widely used as building blocks for UK vocational qualifications and business improvement tools. The standards are developed by groups of employers for their employees through a Sector Skills Council (SSC) or Standards Setting Body (SSB) and the qualifications are often termed National Vocational Qualifications or NVQs. The SSB responsible for the Coaching and Mentoring National Occupational Standards is known as ENTO.

A tangible sign of the increasing cooperation between the existing professional bodies was the creation of the UK coaching bodies Roundtable in 2005. The term 'Roundtable' was agreed as a compromise to protect the aspirations of some of the bodies who feared domination by other bodies. This led to a slow start in achieving the objectives of the Roundtable to work together to maintain the principles on which the various bodies agreed and through which the bodies will operate. Specifically:

- to cooperate to enhance the reputation of the coaching industry;

■ to issue joint statements on issues of shared concern;

■ to discuss the areas where collaboration might be of benefit.

The first area where this collaboration has already seen tangible progress was in 2007 with the publication of 'A statement of shared professional values'. This statement has been drafted and unanimously signed by a group of professional coaching bodies in the UK that have agreed to cooperate to enhance the reputation of the coaching industry.

The following are fundamental principles by which the members are expected to operate.

In the emerging profession of coaching, we believe that:

■ Every coach, whether charging fees for coaching provided to individuals or organizations or both, is best served by being a member of a professional body which suits his/her needs.
■ Every coach needs to abide by a code of governing ethics and apply acknowledged standards to the performance of their coaching work.
■ Every coach needs to invest in their ongoing continuing professional development to ensure the quality of their service and their level of skill is enhanced.
■ Every coach has a duty of care to ensure the good reputation of the emerging profession.

Meta principle

To continually enhance the competence and reputation of the coaching profession.

Principle 1 – Reputation

Every coach will act positively and in a manner that increases the public's understanding and acceptance of coaching.

Principle 2 – Continuous competence enhancement

Every coach accepts the need to enhance their experience, knowledge, capability and competence on a continuous basis.

Principle 3 – Client-centred

Every client is creative, resourceful and whole and the coach's role is to keep the development of that client central to his/her work, ensuring all services provided are appropriate to the client's needs.

Principle 4 – Confidentiality and standards

Every coach has a professional responsibility (beyond the terms of the contract with the client) to apply high standards in their service provision and behaviour. He/she needs to be open and frank about methods and techniques used in the coaching process, maintain only appropriate records and to respect the confidentiality a) of the work with their clients, and b) of their representative body's members' information.

Principle 5 – Law and diversity

Every coach will act within the Laws of the jurisdictions within which they practise and will also acknowledge and promote diversity at all times.

Principle 6 – Boundary management

Every coach will recognize their own limitations of competence and the need to exercise boundary management. The client's right to terminate the coaching process will be respected at all times, as will the need to acknowledge different approaches to coaching which may be more effective for the client than their own. Every endeavour will be taken to ensure the avoidance of conflicts of interest.

Principle 7 – Personal pledge

Every coach will undertake to abide by the above principles which will complement the principles, codes of ethics and conduct set out by their own representative body to which they adhere and by the breach of which they would be required to undergo due process.

Signed by: (in alphabetical order) Association for Coaching, Association of Professional Executive Coaching and Supervision, European Mentoring and Coaching Council – UK, UKICF – The International Coach Federation in the UK

Even more encouraging than this published statement has been the establishment of a joint project in 2008. This involves all four bodies agreeing on definitions, descriptions and standards for the activity widely known as 'supervision,' something which has been imported into coaching and mentoring from several of the 'influencers' professions. We discuss this in more detail later but the fact that genuine dialogue and cooperation has occurred is a tangible step towards the establishment of a real 'profession'.

As well as membership bodies, a requirement to be considered a profession is the identification of different levels or grades of practitioner. A review of the current professional bodies shows that they all have a number of membership grades to identify levels of coaching and mentoring. These levels typically are:

▨ Affiliate – for those interested but not considered as competent.

▨ Associate – for those learning or just starting to develop their competence.

▨ Member – for those considered as competent and experienced.

▨ Fellow – for those who have made a significant contribution or are very competent and very experienced.

The exact descriptions tend to vary, but the above list covers the concept and is transferable across most professions. The requirements for different levels of membership are usually a combination of experience, often expressed as a number of years' proven practice, plus qualification training and ongoing professional education attainment.

4. Qualification requirements

Most professions have a qualification requirement before an individual can achieve full membership of the profession. In the UK, that qualification must be recognized by the government's QCA as well as the profession's membership bodies.

This has posed a problem for some of the emerging professional bodies, which have opted for a process of self-certification of experience (or accreditation) without direct links into the recognized governmental structures and with varying levels of rigour in their training requirements in their 'credentialing' process. In part, this slightly odd term 'credentialing' has been imported from the United States by the ICF, which based its process largely on the US experience. This has led to confusion because most Europeans tend to see accreditation as a post-qualification process to confirm ongoing 'fitness to practice' whereas the ICF process, although very rigorous, can be seen as an alternative to a basic qualification requirement. This confusion is more than a semantic issue and will have to be clarified as the profession matures still further; most probably through the agreement of applying the concept of 'equivalence', which recognizes identical or very similar practices using different words and sometimes differing processes.

Although most of the emerging bodies have a structured approach, the EMCC approach may be instructive in this debate. EMCC initially carried out a three-year worldwide research project to survey all published competency frameworks as the basis for developing its own. This led to a competence framework and associated set of competence statements that suggested six levels of capability:

Foundation Level 3	Equivalent to NVQ 3
Foundation Level 4	Equivalent to NVQ 4
Intermediate Level 5	Equivalent to NVQ 5
Practitioner Level 7	Equivalent to Postgraduate Certificate
Advanced Practitioner Level 7	Equivalent to Postgraduate Diploma
Master Practitioner Level 7	Equivalent to Master's Degree

The EMCC then conducted a further two-year consultation period across the coaching and mentoring community. This led to a reduction in the number of levels and a simplification of the language used to make it more easily understood and applied to the variety of contexts in which coaching and mentoring apply.

This has enabled practising coaches or mentors to 'map' their capability against the various competence levels and statements to establish where they fit within this framework. The competence framework also allows different coaching qualifications and training programmes to be benchmarked against the levels. There is a quality assurance process run across Europe by the EMCC, which has enabled many of the leading training organizations to submit their training programmes to be assessed against any of the six levels.

This carries many benefits relevant to a professional status. It enables potential purchasers of external coaching to compare suppliers on an equal basis. It also helps training organizations to explain which level of capability their qualification equips someone to achieve. This in turn helps someone seeking a qualification or training programme to choose the most appropriate one for his or her current capability and aspirations.

Although there is not one professional 'lead body', this benchmark framework satisfies another requirement of a profession, making it possible to compare different qualifications and coaches and mentors working in different contexts against a common standard. Again, the concept of 'equivalence' will prove to be a unifying instrument to achieve wide acceptance.

Qualifications are available from many suppliers as well as some of the professional bodies that completely or partly cover the competences related to specific levels. This enables anyone to source training or development programmes that will enable him or her to satisfy the education requirements for all the professional levels. Until recently, becoming a qualified coach or mentor required an individual to complete a programme of training or development that carried the appropriate accreditation. However, a process to accredit individuals has been adopted that recognizes that there are many individuals who have developed considerable expertise, and have significant experience as a practising and successful coach and mentor, without undergoing a formal qualification or training programme. This individual accreditation process uses the well-established 'Accreditation of Prior Experience and Learning' or APEL process. The availability of this individual accreditation process to complement the formal accreditation programmes means everyone has access to a suitable qualification.

5. Continuous professional development criteria

All professions expect their members to undergo a continuous programme of professional development, or CPD. This is to ensure their knowledge and skills are kept up to date so that clients can be reassured of the competence of their coach and mentor and their continuing 'fitness to practice'. All the professional bodies described earlier have a measure of CPD criteria built into their membership requirements through their code of ethics and the competence standards.

So once again another requirement of a profession is satisfied. There are a full range of qualifications available and clear statements of the CPD requirements.

THE 'SUPERVISION' DEBATE

Another sign of the maturing nature of the coaching and mentoring profession is the growth of interest in the topic of supervision. Before 2000, the term 'Coaching supervision' hardly existed and was rarely mentioned in any of the coaching manuals. Since then there has been a steadily increasing interest in supervision to the point where every book on coaching, including this one, has to take it into account.

In this section we are going to consider what has led to this growing interest and how it relates to our theme of professionalism. We also hope it will help coaches and mentors consider supervision and how it may apply to their own situation.

Supervision has been an established part of other professions, such as psychotherapy, counselling and nursing, for many years. It is a job requirement for people in these professions to be engaged in supervision on a regular and regulated basis. The National Health Service describes clinical supervision as: 'a formal process of professional support and learning which enables individual practitioners to develop knowledge and competence, assume responsibility for their own practice, and enhance consumer protection and safety of care in complex situations'.

The importance this profession puts on effective clinical supervision is further illustrated by how the Mental Health Nursing Association describes it:

> a dynamic, interpersonally, focused experience promotes the development of therapeutic proficiency. One of the primary reasons for all supervision is to ensure that the quality of therapeutic intervention with the client is of a consistently high standard in relation to the client's needs. Consequently, supervision must be acknowledged as a cornerstone of clinical practice.

We believe that it is not a coincidence that the increase in the number of psychotherapists and psychologists entering the coaching profession coincides with an increase in discussions about coaching supervision. As individuals from these professions move into the coaching environment, it is natural that they will want to bring their established and respected practices with them. It could be argued that it is the psychologists and psychotherapists who are driving the move towards making it a professional requirement for coaches to be 'in supervision'.

At the time of writing, there is a lively debate among professionals about the use of the word 'supervision' in the context of coaching and mentoring. This is because of its connotations with clinical supervision and line management. In many practitioners' views supervision is basically a post-qualification or post-basic training requirement that relates to the ongoing professional development and practice of a coach or mentor to ensure that he or she continues to be competent and up to date with current developments and ideas of 'best practice' in the profession. Thus the debate centres on the need to agree definitions, standards and an alternative and more appropriate term than 'supervision'. Acknowledging that this is an ongoing debate, for simplicity we will continue to use the term 'supervision'.

Self-regulation

It would appear that the case for supervision is being driven by regulatory pressures from a number of the leading players in the profession. The EMCC, as part of its role in bringing the key influencers of the profession together, has stated in its code of ethics that members are required to: 'Maintain a relationship with a suitably-qualified supervisor who will regularly assess their competence and support their development.'

Most of the major professional bodies mentioned earlier have similar expectations of their members to be in regular supervision. However, there are many individuals in the profession who don't need to be 'told' to have supervision. Many coaches, whether they are members of professional institutes or not, see supervision as an essential part of self-development. They seek it out because they know that continuous professional development makes a significant difference to their practice.

Many organizations employ internal coaches to promote coaching as a driver of cultural change, develop a coaching culture, or provide individual coaching for identified employees. Among these internal coaches there is also the recognition of the need for coaching supervision. In this case, the additional organizational drivers are to increase internal capability, standardize approaches and disseminate best practices across the community.

WHAT IS COACHING SUPERVISION?

There seems to be quite a wide spread of opinions when it comes to defining coaching supervision. Bachkirova *et al* (2005) describe it in businesslike terms as: 'a formal process of professional support, which ensures continuing development of the coach and effectiveness of his/her coaching practice through interactive reflection, interpretive evaluation and the sharing of expertise'. Bond and Holland (1998) offer a simpler view: 'Supervision is a regular, protected time for facilitated, in-depth reflection on coaching practice.'

A working party of the four UK professional bodies suggested the following template for concluding the debate about supervision by offering answers to the following key questions.

Q1. What is supervision?

It is a conversational process that helps coaches and mentors to manage their own learning and development in order to improve their ongoing practice. It can be described as a type of CPD that focuses on reflection, insight and support.

Q2. Why should coaches and mentors do it?

Because the process benefits all stakeholder groups involved.

Q3. How should it be done?

There is no single correct way but there are general principles and standards that could act as professional 'best practice' guidelines.

Q4. What should it be called?

There is widespread agreement that it may be desirable to find an alternative to 'supervision' but there is also recognition that it may be very difficult to drop 'supervision' completely. Current suggestions include:

▌ Independent professional development facilitator.
▌ Mentor coach supervisor.
▌ Coach mentor supervisor.
▌ Reflective practice supervisor.

Whatever actual definition is preferred, there appears to be a common agreement that coaching and mentoring supervision is set up to facilitate the ongoing learning and continuous improvement of coaches and mentors. Taking the various definitions into account, we believe the essential elements of effective coaching supervision are:

▎ *Regular sessions* – how often you should have a supervision session is not clear and there do not appear to be any universal standards. One common approach is to link supervision frequency to a specified number of coaching hours. However the frequency is worked out, it is clear that for coaching supervision to be effective it needs to be seen as a regular process.

▎ *Reflection on practice* – the main topic of conversation during a supervision session is on the supervisee's coaching practice. Past experiences are reviewed to extract the learning from the experience to improve future practice.

▎ *Alternative perspective* – the role of the supervisor is more participatory than in many coaching relationships. The supervisor is expected to be more of a mentor, bringing and sharing his or her own experiences, knowledge and understanding to enhance the learning.

▎ *Independent integrity* – the supervisor takes an impartial and external view, acting on behalf of the whole profession and the end client. This enables him or her to hold up the supervisee's behaviour to professional scrutiny and challenge it on occasions and, in some instances, reporting on trends and key issues to a sponsor or professional body.

▎ *Learning focus* – the main purpose of coaching supervision seems to be to facilitate the learning of the supervisee. This is done through a combination of reflection and analysis of past experiences, sharing good practices, and teaching new techniques and theories.

FORMAL OR INFORMAL?

We could argue that, if the key role of a coaching supervisor is to facilitate learning and continuous development for the coach and mentor, this is just what an experienced coach does for his or her clients. A coach does not need to be a subject expert to help learners reflect on their situation. Doesn't a coach enable learners to draw significant learning through active listening and probing questioning?

Many of a coach's needs for support can be met through informal peer supervision between equals, either one-to-one or in groups. This form of relationship will satisfy the need to share experiences and ideas and will also help to reflect on incidents and dilemmas from past sessions. If we believe that peer coaching makes the learning experience richer through the expression of a diversity of views, we can accept that informal peer supervision is a very effective and legitimate form of supervision.

While the intentions of both relationships are the same, we believe the main differences between formal coaching supervision and informal peer coaching or 'coaching the coach' are as follows:

▌ Part of the supervisor's role is that of teacher, so it is expected that the supervisor is more experienced, skilled and/or knowledgeable than the supervisee in specific aspects of coaching and mentoring. The supervisor enhances 'seeing': the seeing into the coaches' practice, the illumination of subtle processes in coaching conversations and of blind spots, deaf spots and dumb spots in themselves and in their thinking.

▌ Coaches in supervision often refer to the relief of having time and space to think about particular aspects of their work and especially to think/reflect with a trusted colleague who will microscopically explore practice with them and contribute to their understanding.

▌ This support enables coaches to contain and resolve some of the more challenging parts of their work, eg:

 – their frustrations with learners;

 – their concern that they are not doing enough;

 – the difficulty of keeping to a coaching contract when the coaching approaches boundaries;

 – the undue influence of the organization (often implicit) or of key stakeholders that might reduce coach effectiveness (power/ disempowerment);

- unexpected emotional material either within the coach or in the learner;

- 'ruptures' in the coaching relationship.

▍ Therefore a supervisor needs a good appreciation of philosophy and psychology to provide this 'super-vision' of the coach's practice.

▍ The supervisor is also expected to represent the profession and uphold the associated ethics, values, standards and policies. The supervisor is therefore effectively playing an independent 'managerial' role. This part of the role provides some level of protection for clients, their purchasing organizations, the provider organizations and the professional bodies.

The expertise and experience needed to effectively carry out these complex roles may be difficult to find in a colleague.

A significant potential weakness of the informal peer supervision is the 'blind leading the blind' or 'we don't know what we don't know'. If the peers in this form of relationship have equal knowledge and experience, where will the learning come from? The quality of the anticipated continuous professional development may suffer without the input from a more skilled and knowledgeable coach-mentoring supervisor.

Another potential weakness is the danger of collusion between peers. Where peers work for the same organization, perhaps in the same department, there is a temptation not to challenge. This may be through wishing to be friends and not upset people, or in support of an internal policy, or in fear of reprisals, or due to other internal politics. In these situations it is felt that only an external supervisor can provide the required independent and objective challenge.

HOW DOES SUPERVISION ADD VALUE?

If there is a case to be made for formal coach mentoring supervision, what are the actual benefits? The best people to answer this important question are coaches and mentors who are receiving supervision for their own benefit. Here are some of the recent (2007) comments from an Oxford School discussion forum of professional coaches asking that very question:

> Sometimes we need a 'back stop', a route to discuss those inevitable dilemmas we face where we are not quite sure how to proceed. Good supervision can clarify our thinking and help us to determine a way forward. It can mitigate any feelings of isolation or even helplessness, giving us confidence, fresh perspectives or perhaps just a reality check.

> It is a mechanism for helping us to develop personally our effectiveness as coaches. It should be a sounding board for testing our skills and abilities and enabling us to improve in such respects. I firmly believe that coaches need coaching too, to avoid us slipping into or perpetuating bad habits.

> It's not just about identifying when we are stuck – you could argue that when we are conscious of an issue we are on the way to resolving it. Supervision is also there to help us pay attention to the elements we are not.

> Supervision helps us to work in a professional fashion and keep within professional boundaries. As an emerging profession we need to have good supervision arrangements in place. For each case of bad practice undermines the credibility of coaching and weakens the case for coaching as a valuable learning experience.

The same group of professional coaches were then asked whether supervision should be a mandatory part of accreditation and continued professional practice. Some thought that it should not be compulsory because, in the words of one coach:

> Any good coach will seek some form of supervision even if it's from their peers. Make it mandatory and it may lack value, becoming another tick in the box, which may not be valued by either the coach or the client.

However, most thought supervision should be a mandatory part of being a professional: 'as much as it is for other people professions but it should equally be entered into voluntarily!'

> Like having a coach, I don't believe that this is an option if we seek to present ourselves to the world as professional coaches. This is a mandatory expense of being involved in the work that we do, in the same way as we register under the Data Protection Act and have professional indemnity insurance.

At this stage in the development of coaching and mentoring, one of the most powerful arguments for formal supervision is that it provides a very effective method of continuous professional development. Therefore, for coaches and mentors who judge themselves to be professionals, we believe they should seriously consider entering a supervision relationship.

Why the reluctance?

If there is a case for practising professional coach-mentors to be in regular supervision, why isn't everyone doing it? In 2006, a survey by the CIPD found that, 'while 86 per cent of coaches responding to our survey believe that coaches should have coaching supervision, only 44 per cent actually do so'.

It appears that many practising coaches and line managers who coach their teams as part of their leadership role do not see the need for formal structured supervision. The reasons given tend to fall into the following categories:

- *Cost:* cannot afford to pay someone to supervise them.
- *Quantity:* do not do enough coaching to make it worthwhile.
- *Context:* only coach 'technical' or 'managerial' skills so don't get into problem emotional areas.
- *Competence:* already know enough and do it well enough, so don't need to go deeper.

From our own experience, we suggest there is a more subtle reason why coaching supervision is not more widespread:

- *Commitment:* there is still a lot of confusion as to what the benefits of coaching supervision actually are, coupled to a general lack of commitment to continuous personal development.

For internal line managers who simply coach their teams as a style of leadership, this view is understandable. Where coaching is seen as only one 'tool' a manager may choose to use with individuals or teams, the need for supervision is difficult to justify. Does a manager need supervision for his or her delegating or other people-handling skills? We would argue that coaching supervision for line managers is an integral part of the role of their own line manager. If managers at all levels adopt a coaching style as their normal management style then they will be practising many of the characteristics of coaching supervision within their line role.

Also, there is considerable evidence that managers, particularly senior managers, learn best in small groups where they can share experiences and discuss ideas and dilemmas with peers in a supportive and challenging environment. Often described as 'action learning sets', these small group meetings could also be described as 'peer coaching supervision'. We believe that, as long as these sessions include and stick to a robust and rigorous learning process, they can provide effective coaching supervision in that context.

So in conclusion, if an organization has established a coaching culture, the need for coaching supervision should be covered by line manager reviews and formally structured action learning or peer coaching sessions. For internal, external and independent coach-mentors, the case for professional coaching and mentoring supervision is becoming clearer and more widespread. For those working in complex, diverse or emotive situations the case is already made by psychologist and author Graham Lee (2007) who summed up the situation admirably when he said:

> Coaches must ensure that their psychological and business skills are kept current through continuing professional development. This typically includes attending conferences, going on courses, reading, and in some cases, making use of a personal coach, counsellor or psychotherapist. However, the most important element of ongoing development for coaches is the use of consultative supervision.

SO, IS IT A PROFESSION OR AN INDUSTRY?

Let us first consider the case against a 'profession'.

Many coaches and mentors are not currently a member of one of the professional bodies described in this chapter. Many do not subscribe to a code of ethics and may not have a formally recognized qualification. We are sure there are many who do not regularly practise CPD or take part in supervision sessions. Many coaches and mentors working in organizations where it is only one part of their role would consider most of this irrelevant or inappropriate to what they do.

There is not a single 'lead body' or dominant professional institute. While there is cooperation between bodies, such as the UK Roundtable, there are significant differences in their philosophy and approach to membership. Also, there is no government regulation for coaches and mentors; they are not required to be a member of a professional body or to have a qualification to practise. A coach or mentor cannot get 'struck off' or banned from practising by any professional body. In the United States there are some early signs that it may be possible to sue a coach for giving wrong advice, but this would be very rare.

However, huge sums of money are being spent by organizations on buying external coaching, and the quantity of people calling themselves coaches or mentors is also significant. So, in terms of quantities and proliferation across both public and private sectors, there is a case to say it is certainly an industry.

A 'profession' or simply 'professional'?

Many people entering the field of coaching and mentoring would consider themselves as professionals moving from other professions. These would include psychotherapists, psychologists, therapists, counsellors, trainers and managers. At present, describing the world of coaching and mentoring as an industry containing many professionals would perhaps be most accurate.

On the other hand, as we have described in this chapter, all the elements for a profession are in place. Historically, most professions have started in a similarly disjointed and piecemeal way. We have noticed an increased momentum in recent years of these discrete components coming closer together. Despite the temptation for some existing professional bodies to absorb and dominate, we believe this convergence will continue to gain momentum both in the UK and across national boundaries. The general acceptance among all stakeholders of the need and desirability of common quality standards, codes of ethics and criteria for continuing professional development may emerge more quickly than a single, or indeed several, powerful professional bodies.

As the title of this chapter suggests, it is our belief that while an industry has been established, a distinct profession is certainly starting to mature.

Appendix: Historical definitions

Various definitions of coaching and mentoring have been advocated over the past 40 years. In chronological order they are as follows:

Mentoring is an essential aid to staff development… which calls for a perspective that looks for future possibilities. This requires a level of trust missing from the judgemental line management relationship where discipline has to be maintained and performance assessed. (Megginson and Baydell, 1979)

Coaching is a process in which a manager, through direct discussion and guided activity, helps a colleague learn and solve a problem, or do a task better than would otherwise have been the case. (Megginson and Boydell, 1984)

There are many views and definitions of the role of mentor, but all include verbs like support, guide, facilitate, etc. Important aspects are to do with listening, questioning and enabling, as distinct from telling, directing and restricting. Mentors are crucial to good management development since they can exert great influence in developing attitudes and encouraging good managerial practice… high quality mentoring is concerned with competence, experience and clear role-definition, but it also crucially depends upon the right balance of personal qualities. (Report by the then Council for National Academic Awards and the Government Training Agency, 1989)

A mentor is a more experienced individual willing to share their knowledge with someone less experienced in a relationship of mutual trust. A mixture of parent and peer, the mentor's primary function is to be a transitional figure in an individual's development.

Mentoring includes coaching, facilitating, counselling and networking. It is not necessary to dazzle the protégé with knowledge and experience. The mentor just has to provide encouragement by sharing his enthusiasm for his job. (Clutterbuck, 1991)

Coaching is the art of facilitating the performance, learning and development of another. Art in the sense that when practised with excellence, there is no attention on the technique but instead the coach is fully engaged with the coachee and the process of coaching becomes a dance between two people moving in harmony and partnership. (Downey, 2003)

Coaching is unlocking a person's potential to maximise their own performance. It is helping them to learn rather than teaching them. (Whitmore, 2003)

Other definitions make slightly different points:

In the modern business context, mentoring is always at least one stage re-moved (from direct line management responsibility), and is concerned with the longer-term acquisition and application of skills in a developing career by a form of advising and counselling. (Parsloe, 1992)

Mentors are people who, through their action and work, help others to achieve their potential. (Shea, 1992)

Whether we label it coaching, advising, counselling or mentoring, if done well its effectiveness will depend in large measure on the manager's belief about human potential. (Whitmore, 1997)

Mentoring is a role which includes coaching, but also embraces broader counselling and support, such as career counselling, privileged access to information, etc. (Landsberg, 1996)

Behind every successful person, there is one elementary truth: somewhere, somehow, someone cared about their growth and development. This person was their mentor. (Kaye, 2002)

By 2004, Clutterbuck had developed his thinking and now described mentoring as an integrating role:

Terms like 'oversee' and 'responsible for' project an image of a hands-on kind of relationship with a clear sense of senior and subordinate. The word 'protégé' also carries distinct overtones of applied power. These concepts are carried on into most of the North American and some European academic literature on mentoring, and in particular, in how mentoring success is measured. It is worth at this point making the controversial but in my view accurate point that the vast majority of US literature on mentoring is of minimal value in planning and understanding mentoring in a European context because it begins from fundamentally different assumptions about the role and nature of mentoring. Mentoring schemes in the UK and Europe, and to a large extent in Australia/New Zealand, tend to conform to a model that emphasises mutuality of learning and the encouragement of the mentee to do things himself or herself; and to a much broader vision of both the role of the mentor and the interactivity between mentor and mentee. (Clutterbuck, 2004)

Here is a more global definition:

Business coaching is the process of engaging in meaningful communication with individuals in businesses, organizations, institutions or governments, with the goal of promoting success at all levels of the organization by affecting the actions of those individuals.

Business coaching enables the client to understand and enhance his or her role in achieving business success. The business coach facilitates client discovery of how personal characteristics, including a sense of self and personal perspectives, affect personal and business processes and the ability to reach objectives within a business context. With this method, successful coaching helps the client learn how to change or accommodate personal characteristics and how to create personal and business processes that achieve objectives.

Business coaching establishes an atmosphere of trust, respect, safety, challenge and accountability to motivate both the coach and the client. In turn, this requires that the business coach conduct an ethical and competent practice, based on appropriate professional experience and business knowledge and an understanding of individual and organizational change.

Clearly the definition includes a range of practice (such as team and individual coaching) within the remit of business coaching but in all aspects the agenda is clearly focused on the achievement of business objectives. It is this focus which delineates business coaching from other types of coaching. Business coaching addresses the development needs of the client required to achieve business outcomes rather than a focus on the personal or career goals of the person being coached. (The World Association of Business Coaches, 2004)

Most recently, in 2008 a UK government sponsored research project into the future skills training needs of coaches and mentors quoted definitions from the Chartered Institute of Personnel and Development:

> [Coaching is] developing a person's skills and knowledge so that their job performance improves, hopefully so that organizational objectives are achieved. Coaching generally occurs over a short duration and is relatively structured to achieve set goals.
>
> [Mentoring is] the passing on of support, guidance and advice in which a more experienced individual uses their knowledge and experience to guide a more junior member of staff. (CIPD, 2008)

References

Adler, N J (2002) Global Companies, Global Society: There is a better way, *Journal of Management Inquiry*, **11**, 3, pp 255–60, selected: 'Editors Choice'

Bachkirova, T, Stevens, P and Willis, P (2005) *Oxford Brookes Coaching and Mentoring Society*, www.brookes.ac.uk

Bandler, R and Grinder, J (1990) *Frogs into Princes: Introduction to Neuro-linguistic Programming*, Eden Grove Editions, London

Berne, E (1973) *Games People Play: The psychology of human relationships*, Penguin, Harmondsworth

Biesser, A (1971) Paradoxical theory of change, in I Fagan and J Shepherd (eds), *Gestalt Therapy Now: Theory, techniques, applications*, HarperCollins College Division, New York

Bond, M and Holland, S (1998) *Skills of Clinical Supervision for Nurses: A practical guide for supervisees, clinical supervisors and managers (Supervision in Context)*, Open University Press, Buckingham

Caplin, J (2003) *Coaching for the Future: How smart companies use coaching and mentoring* CIPD, London

CIPD (2008) in *Everyone Needs a Mentor* (2008) by D Clutterbuck, CIPD, London

Clutterbuck, D (1991, 2004, 2008) *Everyone Needs a Mentor – Fostering talent in your organization*, CIPD, London

Cooperrider, D, Whitney, D and Stavros, J (2008) *Appreciative Inquiry Handbook*, Berrett-Koehler, San Francisco, CA

Council for National Academic Awards and the Government Training Agency (1989) *The Assessment of Management Competencies*, Council for National Academic Awards

Downey, M (2003) *Effective Coaching: Lessons from the coaches' couch*, Texere/Thompson, New York

Flaherty, J (1999) *Coaching: Evoking Excellence in Others*, Butterworth-Heinemann, Oxford

Gallwey, T (1974) *The Inner Game of Tennis*, Random House, New York

Gallwey, T (2000) *The Inner Game of Work*, Random House, New York

Gardner, H, (2006) *Multiple Intelligences: New horizons in theory and practice*, 2nd edn, Basic Books, New York

Goleman, D (1996) *Emotional Intelligence*, Bloomsbury Publishing, London

Grant, A M (2001) *Towards a Psychology of Coaching*, accessed 12 May, 2003, www.psych.usyd.edu.au

Guest, G (1999) *Building Learning Organisations*, paper to the European Consortium of Learning Organisations Conference, Glasgow

Handy, C (2002) *The Age of Unreason: New thinking for a new world*, Random House, New York

Hammond, S A (1998) *The Thin Book of Appreciative Inquiry*, Thin Book Publishing, Bend, OR

Harrison, R (1991, 1998) *People Management*, CIPD, London

Hay, J (1995) *Transformational Mentoring: Creating developmental alliances for changing organisational cultures*, Sherwood Publishing, Watford

Hersey, P, Blanchard, K and Johnson, D (2007) *Management of Organizational Behaviour*, 9th edn, Pearson Education, Oxford

Honey, P and Mumford, A (1986) *Using Your Learning Styles*, Peter Honey Publications, Maidenhead

Jung, C G (1998) *Psychological Reflections: A new anthology*, J Jacobi (ed), Routledge, London

Kaye, B L (2002) *Up is Not the Only Way*, Davies-Black, Mountain View, CA

Kline, N (1999) *Time to Think: Listening to ignite the human mind*, Cassell, London

Landsberg, M (1996) *The Tao of Coaching*, HarperCollins, Toronto, ON

Lee, G (2007) *Leadership Coaching: From personal insight to organizational performance*, CIPD, London

Lucas, B (2001) *Power Up Your Mind: Learn faster, work smarter*, Nicholas Brealey, London

Maddern, J (1994) *Accelarated Learning*, Accelerated Learning Centre, Bristol

Mayo, A and Lank, E (1994) *The Power of Learning: A guide to gaining competitive advantage*, CIPD, London

Megginson, D and Boydell, T (1979, 1984) *A Manager's Guide to Coaching*, British Association for Commercial and Industrial Education, London

Morris, M, Rutt, S and Eggers, M (2004) *Pupil Outcomes: The impact of EIC*, National Foundation for Educational Research, Slough

Mumford, A (1999) *Effective Learning*, CIPD, London

Ofsted (2003) *Excellence in Cities and Education Action Zones: Management and impact*, Ref: HMI1399, Ofsted Publications Centre, London

Parsloe, E (1992) *Coaching, Mentoring and Assessing*, Kogan Page, London

Pease, A and Pease, B (2004) *The Definitive Book of Body Language: The secret meaning behind people's gestures*, Orion, London

Pedler, M (2008) *Action Learning for Managers*, 2nd edn, Gower, Aldershot

Peltier, B (2002) *The Psychology of Executive Coaching: Theory and application*, Brunner-Routledge, London

Rosinski, P (2004) *Coaching across Cultures*, Nicholas Brealey, London

Salovay, P, Brackett, M and Mayer, J (2004) *Emotional Intelligence: Key readings on the Mayer and Salovey model*, National Professional Resources Inc, New York

Sartre, J-P (1943, new translation 1990) *Being and Nothingness: An essay on phenomenological ontology*, Routledge, London

Seligman, M (2005) *Learned Optimism*, Simon & Schuster, New York

Senge, P (1992) *The Fifth Discipline*, Random House, New York

Shea, G F (1992) *Mentoring: A guide to the basics*, Kogan Page, London

Sobolewsha, I (2007) *Coaching Men vs Coaching Women*, Research Paper, SKAI Ltd

Starr, J (2003) *The Coaching Manual*, Pearson Education, Oxford

Thomson, P, Graham, J and Lloyd, T (2005) *A Woman's Place is in the Boardroom*, Palgrave MacMillan, Basingstoke

Tute, W (1995) *People Management*, CIPD, London

Whitmore, J (1987) *The Winning Mind: Strategies for successful sailing*, John Wiley & Sons, Chichester

Whitmore, J ([1997] 2002) *Coaching for Performance*, Nicholas Brealey, London

The World Association of Business Coaches (2004) *Business Coaching Worldwide*, WABC, Canada

Zohar, D and Marshall, I (2001) *Spiritual Intelligence: The ultimate intelligence*, Bloomsbury, London

Index

NB: page numbers in *italic* indicate figures or tables

ALSO AVAILABLE FROM KOGAN PAGE

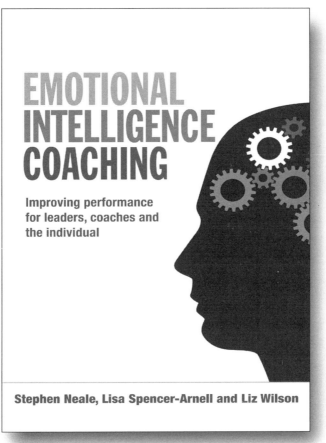

ISBN: 978 0 7494 5458 6   Hardback   2009

Order online now at www.koganpage.com

Sign up for regular e-mail updates on new
Kogan Page books in your interest area

ALSO AVAILABLE FROM KOGAN PAGE